MW00625087

THE WORLD OF STATES

THE WORLD
OF STATES

Connected Essays

J.D.B. MILLER

ST. MARTIN'S PRESS NEW YORK

Library of Congress Cataloguing in Publication Data

Miller, John Donald Bruce.
  The world of states.

  1. State, The—Addresses, essays, lectures.
2. International relations—Addresses, essays, lectures.
3. International organization—Addresses, essays, lectures.   I. Title.
JX4001.M54 1981   341.26   80-22005

ISBN 0-312-89240-3

CONTENTS

For
Barbara and Joe
Stately but more than symbolic.

ABBREVIATIONS

ASEAN	Association of Southeast Asian Nations
CAP	Common Agricultural Policy
CIA	Central Intelligence Agency
COMECON	Council for Mutual Economic Aid
EC	European Community
ECOSOC	UN Economic and Social Council
ECSC	European Coal and Steel Community
EEC	European Economic Community
FAO	Food and Agriculture Organization
GATT	General Agreement on Tariffs and Trade
IBM	International Business Machines
ICAO	International Civil Aviation Organization
ILO	International Labour Organization
NATO	North Atlantic Treaty Organization
NIEO	New International Economic Order
OAU	Organization of African Unity
OECD	Organization for Economic Cooperation and Development
OEEC	Organization for European Economic Cooperation
OPEC	Organization of Petroleum Exporting Countries
UNCSTD	United Nations Conference on Science and Technology for Development
UNCTAD	United Nations Conference on Trade and Development
UNESCO	United Nations Educational, Scientific and Cultural Organization

PREFACE

This book is about the sovereign state in its international capacity, especially its chances of survival. I am particularly interested in suggestions that the state is outmoded as an institution, and will be superseded in various ways by other bodies. Ideas of this sort have been common in recent years in writings about international politics, mainly in the United States, but also in other countries.

The essays approach the issue somewhat indirectly by examining the specific notions that diplomacy is outmoded, integration imminent and interdependence a vast force for change in states and international organisations. There is also an essay on the contemporary sovereign state's significance for its citizens, and one on Australia, the state I know best. Essay 5 attempts to bring together some of the aspects of politics and economics in the international sphere.

While the treatment is episodic, the message, I hope, is clear: that sovereign states are here to stay, because there is no viable alternative. International organisations are, to a striking extent, their playthings, and multinational corporations ultimately subject to their control, unless the state in question is very weak and very poor. Diplomacy has much the same characteristics as in the past, although many of the conditions in which it operates have changed.

Two of the essays are on somewhat broader topics though related to the others. Essay 1 is an account of how I think the international system should be analysed, at least in the first instance. Essay 9 deals with the numerous ironic situations which occur in the relations between states.

Part of Essay 2 has been published before. It was my inaugural lecture at the Australian National University on 17 September 1963. Essay 6 has some ideas from my Arthur Pool Memorial Lecture, given at the University of Leicester on 28 February 1978, and printed in University of Leicester Convocation Review 1978. Two other essays began as seminar papers in the department in which I work. I am grateful to my colleagues for their criticisms.

The last three essays were written in China — in Peking and Chungking, and on the boat from Chungking to Wuhan. My companions from the academies of the Social Sciences and the Humanities in

Australia are to be saluted for their encouragement and sympathy.

I am most grateful to Coral Bell, Martin Indyk and Toby Miller for comments on the drafts they received. My own stubbornness must be held responsible for any errors of fact and judgement which remain. Lynn McLeod deserves my thanks for her prompt and accurate typing.

My wife Margaret has shared the making of books with me for over twenty-five years. My gratitude is inexpressible, but is recorded here with love.

J.D.B.M.

1 THE POLITICS OF INTERNATIONAL RELATIONS

The world of states is the world we live in. For better or worse, it is what the human race has made of its condition. Whether we like it or not, no one can say with any confidence that a world of states is unnatural, any more than a covey of partridges or a pride of lions. As we shall see, there has been much speculation about whether the number of states is likely to be reduced by integration between some of them, and about the effect on states of the increasing interdependence which they experience; but the central fact of the organisation of mankind is still the sovereign state, and there is reason to believe that people want more from the state rather than less.

In this book we shall be concerned with the behaviour of states towards one another, and with whether the state, as a form of social organisation, is likely to continue. The first of these two problems is the more important, although its future is likely to be very much affected by the second. However, there are also problems in how we approach the study of state behaviour. These problems arise partly from arguments between academics, who cannot contain themselves when questions of definition arise, but also from the inherent difficulties of the situation which we need to examine. So far as the problems of academic differentiation are concerned, I have always found these unreal; the people discussing them have quarrelled bitterly over whether to call their study 'international relations', 'international politics' or 'world politics', but have usually finished up by talking about the same things even though they used different words to describe them. It is as if a group of elephant keepers held a series of solemn meetings to discuss what elephant keeping would be like if there were such things as elephants, and spent the time between meetings in looking after elephants.

Yet there is some significance in the choice between 'international relations' and 'international politics', to the extent that the first term may enable us to evade the important questions of whether international relations are political, and, if so, what is politics. One could effectively describe the activities of states without answering these questions, but one could not connect them, in any systematic way, with the activities of

1

politicians as we normally understand them; and it is politicians who decide state policy, whether in Moscow, Washington, London, Teheran or Canberra.

The commonsense approach is that, since the activities with which we are most concerned in studying the relations between states (i.e., aspects of foreign policy) are the actions of politicians, they must be political, especially since they are carried on within the same context of state authority as other actions of the same politicians. The more interesting question, however, is what the international activities have in common with the domestic activities.

To decide this, one needs a framework of analysis which connects the two. I think that the same sort of analysis can be used for both, since both are essentially political, not simply because they proceed from the actions of politicians but because they arise from the same basic circumstances.

I

This view of politics rests upon three concepts which I call inequality, interests and government. Each requires explanation, which, in the first place, will be provided in domestic terms.

Inequality in this context is really another name for scarcity, which lies also at the root of economics. Just as, by definition, there would be no economics if everyone had all that he wanted, so there would be no politics if everyone had what he wanted — or, to put it another way, if everyone were equal and were satisfied with this equality since it included all that he could possibly want. In fact, of course, there is not and never has been enough to go round however we define what it is that has to go round. 'Goods and services' is a fair enough definition for economics to work upon when it deals with what people want; but in politics we have to think not only in terms of the things one can buy, but also of conditions of life which produce satisfying states of mind, such as personal freedom, national identity and a number of other aspects of life. These cannot be costed in financial terms, but can bulk large in political demand. Inequality, which for my purposes can also be called diversity,[1] is the motive force behind political action: it is not an inevitable source of motivation, but it is the normal source of what, in the jargon of today, is called 'politicisation' — that is, the state of mind in which one seeks political solutions to one's problems; in which, it could be said, one's search for advantage is specifically political, in the sense that it is directed towards solutions to be achieved through government.

That search is normally carried on in company with other people; this is where the concept of interests comes in. An interest is that which binds people together. In practical terms the word can also be used to describe the group of people who have a common concern which they wish to pursue. Thus one can speak of 'interests', in the plural, to mean both the attitudes of mind which characterise groups of people with common concerns, and the groups themselves. We speak of 'interests' in any given society, as those groups which pursue their collective advantage through contact with government.

'Government' is the third of the concepts necessary to basic political analysis. 'Government' means the official power, the authorities. Sometimes, in fact, 'authority' would be a better word. It does not have to be 'sovereign', in the traditional sense, to constitute official power; power can have been delegated to it, and it can be quite limited in its range. What is important is that it should be the authority which, in a given situation, interests need to influence or control in order to achieve what they want.

Thus interests come into existence because of inequality (or relative scarcity, if one prefers), and attempt to influence government or authority to their advantage. This is the basic system of analysis which, in any given political situation, enables us to see what is happening, and to judge what may happen next.

It is important to recognise that each of the three concepts — inequality, interests and government — is capable of further refinement. As already indicated, inequality is essentially comparative but eternal just the same; what will be regarded as a politically significant form of inequality in one place, capable of arousing political consciousness and creating an articulate political movement, may be insignificant in another place — though we may be sure that other inequalities or diversities will be important there, and will, given the opportunity, arouse a similar reaction.

The use of that phrase, 'given the opportunity', indicates that the third concept, 'government' is also capable of further refinement and of considerable variation. There are all sorts of governments or authorities. They are distinguished, not only by the extent to which they exercise sovereignty, but also by differing degrees of coercive power and disregard for the opinions of their peoples. This means that in some places it is much easier for interests to express themselves than in others. In China, for example, there are great difficulties in expressing disagreement with official policy. All the same, divergent interests do exist; their activities must, however, be largely indirect in character, and their existence usually becomes clear after they have achieved something — or failed to achieve it — within the government itself. Anything further from the strident articulation of interests in the United States would be difficult to imagine; yet the function performed — that of people with a common concern striving to affect the decisions of government — is the same. What is different is the scope of opportunity, and the methods which need to be adopted because of the nature of the governmental system.

'Interests' is also capable of much variation. To constitute an interest, a group of people does not need to be organised, to have a constitution, an office, a secretary and the like; it can be simply a number of people with imperfect communications between them who act together from time to time. Indeed one can even speak of a 'latent interest', in the sense of a group of people whose common concern might be awakened in favourable circumstances, but who, in the meantime, may not even know of one another's existence, or may be separated by other attitudes of mind which seem more important for the time being. For purposes of analysis, this is dangerous ground; one sees, far too often, attempts at analysis which state baldly that 'the workers' or 'the coloured peoples' or 'business' or 'the intellectuals' will say or do such and such, when in fact they prove to have no uniting principles. Yet it is necessary to preserve the notion of latent interests for possible use, just as it is to recognise that in politics at certain times the decisive action is taken not by groups but by individuals. In these cases one can retain the original framework of analysis by asserting that individuals, however gifted and charismatic, will not survive for long in politics unless interests form up behind them, or they attach themselves to existing interests.

Perhaps the only other major qualification to introduce is that the advantage which interests seek does not need to be solely material; it can also be ideological, altruistic or whatever other term one chooses to describe the conviction that something beyond goods and services is worth pursuing. Goods and services, however satisfying as the postulated goal of economic activity, will not suffice to describe the goals of political activity. They are always somewhere in the picture, but it is unwise to assume that they are all that matters.

Politics, then, is a universal human activity, found wherever there are inequality and some form of government — that is to say, everywhere. It is pursued by individuals and by groups which I call interests, but acquires its main force from the formation and persistence of interests. It is never likely to stop.[2]

II

The question now is whether this sort of analysis, expressed in terms of the domestic politics of any given state, is also applicable to what we variously call international politics or international relations, or whether there is something generically different about that sort of activity.

There is not much difficulty in accepting two of the concepts, those of inequality and interest. Inequality between states in resources, power and living standards is a commonplace in discussions of international politics, and is widely accepted as a reason for conflict. If we are not talking about differences between the industrialised countries and the Third World, we are examining the rush for colonies in the nineteenth century or the search for gold in the sixteenth; and if we are not asserting that states wish to take territory from one another, we are likely to say that their sense of insecurity is such that they take defensive measures which in turn create military inequalities which exacerbate the political situation. We are well aware of the intense diplomacy between contemporary states over tariffs, markets, rates of exchange, economic aid, investment and so on. Inequality is the prime fact of international life; if it is not seen in these material terms, it is seen in differential access to those human rights which are so often talked about but so little practised. One can subsume under 'inequality' or 'scarcity' a great many, perhaps all, of the sources of division and hostility amongst great powers and small. One can even say, with some justice, that, since there can never be complete and permanent equality of power between states (however power is measured), there is always likely to be suspicion and mutual fear.

Similarly, 'interests' are not difficult to accommodate within our understanding of international politics. We are accustomed to speak of 'national interests', meaning those things which states strive to preserve and enhance, sometimes to the point of war. We also speak of 'common interests' or a 'coincidence of interests' between a group of states, in order to explain their acting together. We recognise, quite often, that these interests are not fully pre-ordained, but depend to a considerable extent on the subjective judgements of governments and public opinion at a particular time. It is thus quite easy, in terms of international politics, to approximate individual states (comprising large numbers of individual persons) and groups of states to those groups of individual people within the domestic politics of a given country which I previously called 'interests'. Like groups within a country, they can be more or less organised and persistent in what they do. The important thing is that the sense of a common concern which impels political action should be present. For international politics, also, the use of 'interests' has the advantage that it does not imply that the only actors are sovereign states. It can accommodate the fashionable (though by no means new) notion that various 'transnational' bodies, from the International Red Cross and the Roman Catholic Church to groups of terrorists and IBM, have a place on the international political scene.

The difficulty comes with the third concept, 'government'. Here a critic is likely to say that there is no direct correspondence between domestic and international politics, since there is no international government. One cannot therefore assert that interests strive to affect the decisions of government; apart from the fact that the major interests are themselves governments, there is no universal authority to which they can appeal, or which can decide anything at all. There is only a notional empty chair, marked, as it were, 'Government of the World'.

This is an important criticism, but in my view it does not invalidate the use of the three concepts as guides to analysis in the international field. This is because the criticism rests upon a view of government which is essentially legalistic in character and does not fully encompass what actually takes place. It is a view which one could call ultra-Austinian, since it assumes a determinate superior or sovereign in all domestic situations, and implies, if it does not assume, that this sovereign makes all the important decisions.[3] This view is realistic when we are concerned with ultimate decisions of state, such as those involving peace and war, but it is not realistic about a great deal of what else goes on in domestic politics.

We can think, for example, of many of the deliberations and agreements between government departments; of the arrangements between nationalised industries and their staffs and suppliers; of the agreements arrived at between departments on the one hand, and professional bodies on the other; of the relations between levels of government in a federation; of the internal management of political parties; of the connections between foreign offices, intelligence services and armed forces in deciding external policy; of the administration of social services; or the allocation of contracts or foreign-aid programmes. These are all political. They are all matters for which one can find final approval by the alleged sovereign if one looks hard enough; but approval is to be found normally in a law passed long before, or in some prerogative power, or in rubber-stamp approval by an overworked minister who may not know what he is signing. In none of these cases can one say that a specific decision has been taken at the highest level. Instead, there have been negotiation, compromise and some sort of decision at lower levels of the process of government between both public and private interests.

The emphasis is essentially on the process rather than on any ultimate authority, upon the relative independence of those involved and upon the interests of the groups as seen by themselves, rather than on continual surveillance by some authority above and beyond them. Politics is invincibly pluralist; there are normally more interests than can be satisfied, and 'the government' itself comprises a whole set of these, often incompatible in many respects, and capable of being reconciled only by processes of log-rolling, back-scratching and the like. Earlier, I used the term 'the authorities' and 'authority' as synonyms for 'government'. They are useful because they highlight the fact that one has to look for different authorities at different times. This is a difficult point for people with British traditions to accept, because of the long supremacy of cabinet government, with its formal assumption that all important matters are finally settled by the cabinet itself; but any close study of memoirs will show how false the assumption is in practice.

My point is that, although some decisions in any domestic system are made by a determinate sovereign, most of them are not; and yet those other decisions are just as much political as the first, being made in what are universally regarded as political contexts, however one takes the word 'political'. The essence of the situation is not the presence of a determinate sovereign, but the existence of a number of largely independent official bodies and of groups of people which embody specific interests, which have some measure of authority and which are capable of influencing the machinery of government to their advantage.

This system or process is very close to what happens in international politics, the essence of which is negotiation between largely independent states in the pursuit of their interests. When states negotiate, they have much in common with the major industrial and bureaucratic interests present in any developed modern state, or the ethnic interests present in these and in so many underdeveloped ones. It is true that in the long run their arguments can be settled for the time being by war, and that war has no direct counterpart in domestic politics, Northern Ireland and terrorist movements notwithstanding; but this may often, though not always, be a distinction without a difference. Most of what happens in international politics is like most of what happens in domestic politics and can be analysed in much the same way. Inequality begets interests which seek their objectives through government — which in the international sphere is authority, represented by the agreements and understandings arrived at by sovereign states.

One can even assert that there is something like the determinate sovereign in the background. In most historical periods one can discern a rough hierarchy of order amongst the states involved in international politics. Some are bigger and more powerful than others, and can exercise influence when they care to. These may at times exercise what amounts to sovereign power, to the extent that they can compel or coerce certain lesser states to do as they wish, and those lesser states habitually obey them. They become, in effect, the authorities. In the nineteenth century the loose systems of Congress and Concert enabled the major European powers to perform something like this function. Today there is a vague kind of overall supervision by the United States and the Soviet Union, which is the reality of the 'hegemony' about which the Chinese so often complain. This hegemony is defective and intermittent; but so too, in any realistic analysis, are the operations of most allegedly sovereign governments in respect of many of the domestic interests which they are assumed to control.

I am not trying to suggest that in any legal sense there is an international sovereign comparable to domestic sovereigns. This would be absurd. Instead, I am saying that in most political situations, in a domestic context such as the American or British or Australian, the so-called sovereign power is often masked or absent, while in most international contexts, although there may be no formal sovereign power, there may well be ultimate authority embodied in great powers which approximate to it. More important, both the domestic and international contexts normally display a broad though vulnerable consensus about how negotiations should be carried on, about which demands border on the outrageous, about which interests are to be recognised as legitimate, about what kinds of pressure are to be tolerated, and so on. None of this consensus is eternal, and much is likely to be discarded under stress. But, as in most domestic contexts, there is a certain minimum of agreed order in the international system.[4]

What we have in that system is machinery in process, which to a large extent provides the justification for its own existence. Like similar domestic machinery, it has a form of sovereignty somewhere in the background, exercising ultimate authority in certain circumstances; but most of the time it functions effectively in its own right, as a set of more or less formalised institutions, without the need for an ultimate authority over the world, or for much interference on the part of individual states. The more technical the matters being discussed — and a great deal of what is actually discussed between states is very technical indeed — the more likely it is that the interests of the states will be accommodated within a framework of broad consensus. It is plain how successfully the world's navigation, meteorology, posts and telegraphs have been promoted through such a process.

III

What then is the nature of international politics?

It arises out of inequality and diversity between states in terms of resources, development, ideologies and standards of living. Because states do not live to themselves, but have common frontiers with others, trade with others and have a variety of other forms of intercourse with them, there is awareness of this inequality at the levels of governmental power, and at times a determination to alter the condition of inequality wherever possible. This is what lies behind trade negotiations, aid programmes, arguments over racial discrimination and the ideological distinctions between communist and capitalist states. Perhaps 'inequality' is not the most suitable term in this latter case, and 'diversity' should be called into play. No inevitable clash or conflict arises from inequality and diversity as such, but one can recognise potential conflict in each instance. The fact that each country expresses its desire to mitigate inequality through a government, through the machinery of a state, gives the operation a special intensity, perhaps an extra dimension. Whereas in domestic contexts the recognition in politics of inequalities usually depends upon the efforts of trade unions, political parties and other such bodies — efforts which may be nullified by contrary forces or by these bodies' own weakness of organisation — in an international context the inequalities are espoused by states. States have position and influence, derived from their very existence and to some extent from the recognition of their legitimacy by other states. There is an extra articulacy, an extra edge, to the efforts of states as interests.

Thus the interests which states espouse have, in many respects, a persistence and a sharpness which interests do not always display in a domestic context. At the same time, however, there is an impermanence about them, since they often depend upon the existence of a particular regime, are bound up with it and may perish with it. There are some state interests which do not change, however. These have given us the notion of permanent national interests, with its concurrent assumption that *all* national interest are permanent. Nothing could be further from the truth. That invincible pluralism mentioned earlier ensures that some interests expressed by states will change with an election or a new dictator. At the same time, many will survive.

Government, the third concept I employ to distinguish the nature of international politics, can be used to describe the actors in diplomacy and the process of diplomacy itself, though 'authority' is a better word in this context. If we think of the states involved in international negotiation as comparable to the various groups, official and unofficial, involved in the kind of negotiation which has political results domestically, we can also think of the international system at large as achieving consensus of a kind, and as having authority exercised by the major powers, in something like the same way as sovereign bodies — monarchs, parliaments, peoples — are said to exercise it in local contexts.

International politics is a ceaseless struggle, but it is not ceaselessly a matter of destruction, any more than domestic politics. Consensus can come about from time to time within the international system. Even if it is not achieved between every state that exists, it can certainly come about between groups of states. As in domestic politics, it is folly to think that everyone will agree about everything. All we can hope for domestically, in realistic terms, is that enough people will agree on the basis of the particular governmental system for long enough to enable it to establish and sustain itself. Such systems can, of course, also be sustained by force; but this needs to have consensus mixed with it, or otherwise the system is likely to collapse.

Here, again, there is a close correspondence with much of what happens in international politics. Just as we can distinguish regimes or governmental systems within the history of a particular country, and see them collapse or be massively changed from time to time as political forces within the country alter, so we can see the international system take different shapes at different times, the major changes often emerging from war. The Napoleonic wars, the Franco-Prussian war, the two world wars of this century, all heralded massive changes throughout the system. In each case a new hierarchy of power emerged, in its turn to be modified by later events, involving shifts in either military or economic strength, or in both.

I do not think that the existence of war, vile though it is, negates the correspondence between domestic and international politics. It is easy to make a sharp contrast between a well-policed country and a world at war and say that the politics they represent have nothing in common; but this is surely an extreme interpretation. In fact, most countries are not well policed, but suffer numerous riots, coups and other forms of civil strife; and in fact most wars are limited in range and do not last as long as some civil commotion. If we regard politics as encompassing violence, since clearly violence of the kind we are discussing involves both interests and governments, then war, the supreme use of violence to express interests, is a political act, and can be regarded as having a political function akin to the violence used by insurrectionary forces within states. It speeds change by asserting the demands of interests which cannot get what they want by the normal processes of representation and negotiation. It is anti-human, but political none the less. If revolution is political, then so is war. It is unwise, however, to regard war as typical of politics between states, any more than we regard violence as typical of politics within them. The threat of violence has a role in many states' politics, just as the threat of war has internationally. We should be foolish not to recognise this. But we should also recognise that most politics at home is a matter of the peaceful accommodation of interests, often to their mutual benefit, and that the same is true abroad.

IV

Let us consider now the objections likely to be brought against the approach to international politics described here.

First, it might be suggested that the approach is too limited in range. To reduce politics (international or not) to inequality, interests and government is to suggest a uniformity which is itself spurious, and which is in any case confined to a narrow range of ideas and activities. In other words, the bases of analysis are too few and are inadequate.

The answer is that, while the terms of analysis are limited, each of them is capable of variation and extension. As indicated earlier, inequality, interests and government are very broad categories which can be given appropriate content in any particular political situation. The essential point is not whether they are few in number but whether they are too few. I have sometimes been tempted to add *location* to them as a further concept, since the spatial distribution of political interests is obviously of great importance in all countries (especially those of large size such as the United States, Canada and Australia) and the physical location of states is of even greater importance when one is considering the international scene. I think, however, that the notion of location need not become a major concept in political analysis, but is better utilised as one of the means of identifying interests, both actual and latent.

Second, another criticism might be that the approach is too broad, in the sense that the three concepts can be made to include everything. They encourage the student to call anything an 'interest' that seems to have any contact at all with government; they dignify as 'government' anything that seems to have influence. When applied to international politics, they equate one country with another as each possessing 'interests', thus encouraging the notion of equality between states and neglecting the realities of power.

The approach is certainly broad, but, if one admits that the three concepts are sufficient for basic analysis, then broadness may be an advantage. If, as analysts, we are aware that any given political situation must embody inequality, interests and government, we will know that none of these can be omitted or neglected, and will look for each one until it is found. The fact that the categories are broad makes it possible to search for detail and complexity within each one. For example, in a situation such as relations between the ASEAN states and those of Indochina, the inequalities arise in the spheres of military power, economic strength, connection with major powers and superpowers, and ideological intensity. The interests are those of the ruling groups in each country in the area, and of those beyond it which are directly concerned, such as the USA, China, the Soviet Union, France and Japan. The authority involved is that complex of relationship between China, the Soviet Union and the USA which is affected by harmony or lack of it within the Association of Southeast Asian Nations (ASEAN), within Indochina and between the two groups of minor states. The superpowers constitute, as it were, the ultimate authorities; but Vietnam and Indonesia, to a lesser extent, represent actual or incipient authority in a military sense, while Japan has it in an economic sense. To the extent that there is struggle within Indochina, or between the ASEAN and the Indochinese states, it is in order to gain either authority within the area (directly or through some future structure of alliance, trade, consultation etc.), or special status with the ultimate authorities.

A third criticism might be that the approach is too amoral and analytical, that it does not condemn inequalities, or recognise differences of worth between interests, or distinguish between good and bad governments. This is true. I do not think morality has a place in political analysis, though it is of major importance in political judgement. The analyst is concerned to establish what is the case, how things work, and, if possible, what will happen next. This will involve consideration of whether interests and governments are stable, how persistent inequalities seem to be, and whether interests will continue to respond in the same way. Whether he likes the interests or not is another story. He may proceed to tell that story after he has done the analysis.

Fourth, one might say that the approach is too political, i.e., that it does not take account of economic and social forces. To me this is like saying that an economic analysis is too economic, or a sociological one too social. If we admit that some activities can properly be regarded as economic and some as political, then the principal analysis will be in economic and political terms respectively. Such a procedure will not prevent us from taking account of other influences in deciding what is happening to the economy or polity in question; but the terms we use will be either economic or political, not both at once. In a political analysis according to my three concepts, the inequalities may well be seen as economic in nature or origin, and the interests as seeking economic ends; but this is no reason for concealing or omitting the political process and effects, which are of principal concern to a political analyst.

V

To conclude, what direct relevance does this form of analysis have to the study of specifically international politics?

In the first place, there is genuine relevance in the emphasis on inequalities and interests. The formal equality between states, on which the diplomatic system is based, is a reality in itself, and must always be recognised as such. (It constitutes, as it were, a morsel of government within the international system.) But the more significant reality, in most situations, is that of the inequality of states. Even within an alliance such as NATO, or an association such as OAU or ASEAN, where the emphasis is placed on formal equality between friends, the inequalities count for most. The fact that they are often subtle rather than blatant, that they express themselves in cultural and ideological rather than military and economic terms, does not make them less real.

There are real difficulties, of course, in estimating the effects of inequalities in creating interests. One can easily be so impressed by obvious inequalities as to presume that an interest is clearly present. The prime example of the moment is the presumed common interest of underdeveloped countries in relation to developed ones. As indicated above, the idea of latent interests is important for analysis, but more as a means of foreshadowing possible change than as a medium of observation of current reality. We can see that the underdeveloped countries agree upon a common interest within the confines of UNCTAD and the UN General Assembly (i.e., within one area of 'government'), and that they have strong latent interests in preserving this solidarity in other contexts, especially economic contexts. We can also see, however, that in the more important area of 'government', that of the major powers, they often pursue individual interests to the point at which a common interest is destroyed. These individual interests arise from the basic inequalities between underdeveloped countries, especially in terms of natural endowment.

The form of analysis suggested here encourages awareness of inequalities, and expectation of diversity of interests, in any international situation. In doing so, it fulfils an important requirement in the social sciences, the need to distinguish analysis from advocacy, and, in particular, to distinguish between actuality and what interested parties (in our case, governments and ideological movements) say is true. To combat illusion and obfuscation is a major task of the scholar in any area of study, especially in those in which propaganda is inseparable from the normal rhetoric.

There is further relevance to international politics in the emphasis on government — not, in this case, because it emphasises the continued significance of the state in international relations, but because it highlights the need to discover the significant elements of authority in any international situation. As indicated above, they are hard to find, and there is likely to be continual argument about them, since they do not respond to the normal enquiries about constitutional provisions. But if we think of them as the governing aspects of constraint and opportunity imposed by the character of the international system at any given time, and look for them in the behaviour of major powers, of neighbours and of international organisations, we shall be in a position to decide how the interests of given states are likely to be affected.

Giving stress to government as inextricably linked with all political situations seems especially important if the government is hard to find. Utopianism was not simply a devil of the 1920s and 30s, exorcised for all time by E.H. Carr;[5] it is a persistent tendency in all discussions of international relations, manifesting itself now in the notion of potential strength in international organisations which do not possess it, now in the postulate of unity amongst allies who are in fact disunited, now in the idea of consistent policy on the part of great powers which in practice vacillate from one position to another and now in the imagined purposive action of Third-World states which care little for one another. The search for government in the international system can be something of an antidote to these excesses, because it involves the idea of constraint as well as that of opportunity. There are likely to be authorities; who are they and how will they behave? Like authorities in any domestic context, they have interests too.

It is also relevant that the form of analysis outlined here can be used by those who maintain that states are the only actors in international politics, and also by those who wish to include a number of unofficial actors such as multinational corporations. It can even be employed by those who enlarge the international spectrum to include the lateral extension of classes from one state to another, though they would probably find it an intolerable burden. All of the actors in question can be regarded as 'interests'; their interaction with one another, and with whatever elements of 'government' are present, constitutes the international politics of any given time. There is still the task, however, of gauging the nature of the inequalities, the intensity and persistence of interests and the conformation and strength of whatever is identified as government.

In subsequent essays, efforts will be made to illustrate further the complexities of the world of states, and how these can be reduced to a certain order by using the broad system of analysis which comprises inequality, interests and government. First, however, it is desirable to deepen our awareness of the significance, in contemporary terms, of the sovereign state.

Notes

1. 'Diversity' was the term used in my book *The Nature of Politics*, first published in 1962 by Duckworth. Since then, I have come to believe that 'inequality', which was used in the first draft of the book, is to be preferred, though both are helpful in clarifying the position.

2. The analysis of politics described here is not solely applicable to those states normally called 'democratic'. It is equally applicable to allegedly monolithic or totalitarian states, since 'interests' do not have to be confined to formal interest-groups as understood in contemporary writings on political science, or 'government' be restricted to the to-and-fro processes of parliaments and elections. The analysis is, again, readily applicable to private politics, such as the politics of a business corporation or a hospital, just as it is to bureaucratic politics, i.e., the politics of a government department or a public corporation. The emphasis is on the perpetual presence of diverse interests within a given framework of authority.

3. I do not mean to be unfair to John Austin, who has suffered from being made the emblem of a particularly inflexible view of law. In fact, he was much more sensitive to the nuances of rule-making than is often supposed. See, in particular, his references to 'positive morality' in Lecture V of *The Province of Jurisprudence Determined*, introduced by H.L.A. Hart (London, 1954).

4. The point has been developed with great clarity and detail by Hedley Bull in *The Anarchical Society*, (London, 1977).

5. E.H. Carr, *The Twenty Years Crisis 1919-1939* (London, 1939).

2 THE SIGNIFICANCE OF THE SOVEREIGN STATE

When we contemplate the world in its political aspect, we are liable to use terms such as 'international society', 'the international community', 'the society of states' or 'the state system' to describe what we see. We can, of course, talk of 'mankind' or 'the family of man' as constituting 'one world', but in doing so we are talking about something that goes beyond politics. (This does not mean that nobody uses such terms in political discussion. When people do, however, it is usually the case that they have particular portions of mankind in mind, and are trying to secure advantage for these.) In most political contexts, we are likely to turn to one of the first four terms or something like it. This is because the 'society', 'community' or 'system' we are talking about is composed of states, not of individuals. States are the principal actors in world politics. It is of them and of other corporate bodies, rather than of individual persons, that the world is made.

I

Sometimes we call them 'sovereign states', to emphasise their formal independence from one another. I do not propose to argue about what constitutes sovereignty in international affairs; this is usually an arid exercise, though sometimes it can be constructive.[1] Just as we know a camel or a chair when we see one, so we know a sovereign state. It is a political entity which is treated as a sovereign state by other sovereign states. There can, of course, be argument about particular cases — e.g., about whether Rhodesia was a sovereign state after it made its unilateral declaration of independence, or Taiwan before and after a number of other states ceased to treat it as China — but these are far less important than the fact that there are now some 150 universally recognised sovereign states, and that their number shows no sign of diminishing. They are the basic units of international politics. No one would suggest that they can be totally separated from their populations, and that, in some sense, there are really no people in the world, only states; but it is fair to say that, while the governments of particular countries are constantly influenced by popular feelings, attitudes and choices, the impact of those countries on others, at any given time, is essentially of them as *states* — as interests in themselves.

More serious and more persistent than arguments about what constitutes a sovereign state are arguments about whether the state as such is a good thing, or whether it should be replaced by some other political arrangement. There are several common complaints against the sovereign state, which are as follows:

First, it is said to encourage war. Since wars are mostly waged between sovereign states (apart from civil and guerrilla wars), some people have maintained that, if there were fewer states or none at all, there would be less likelihood of war. The essence of the state's sovereignty is its claim to do as it sees fit, subject to the cloudy and often contradictory demands of international law; if mankind were not divided up into states, or if, at the least, the states which existed were subject to some control by an overall body acting in the interests of mankind, wars would not occur. The state's implicit claim to use war as an instrument of policy is sometimes likened to the use of violence in their own interests by gangs of criminals. Effective policing is said to be the remedy in both cases.

Second, the state is seen as a hindrance to a proper division of labour throughout the world, since sovereign states, in pursuit of economic advantage for their own peoples, claim the right to restrict the movement of workers and capital and to prevent the free flow of goods and services from where they can be most efficiently produced to where they are most wanted. The world is thus prevented from operating as a single economy in which supply and demand could come to the best terms.

Third, the state is pilloried because it hinders the appearance of more appropriate political units. It is argued by some of the writers quoted in Essay 5 that, with the growth of technology in modern communications and transport, existing state boundaries are often inadequate to represent the areas of interest which unite particular groups of people. Regions, continents and sometimes the world as a whole, are suggested as alternatives because such influences as economic interdependence, ecological unity and the common danger from nuclear weapons, demand political units larger than those represented by most states.

Fourth, as a related criticism, the state is said to encourage a sense of particularity when a sense of unity is required. Instead of people confining their loyalty to a sovereign state, it is held that they should look for the fulfilment of their aspirations towards larger entities such as their continents (e.g., 'Europe' or 'Africa'), and that in matters of major concern they should look to mankind. This kind of criticism, unlike the second and third, is not based upon technological change or the maximisation of economic advantage, but upon the idea of a common human heritage, either with those located within a particular land-mass or with the human race as a whole.

These criticisms all deserve respect. Further reference will be made to them elsewhere in this book. For the moment, however, it is sufficient to state them and to reiterate that, in spite of them, we still have sovereign states, and that the number continues to increase. The object of all the so-called 'nationalist movements' of the world since World War II has been the creation of more sovereign states. The nature and record of the state as an institution appear to encourage those who seek independence to claim it as their birthright. In the latter half of the twentieth century this urge has been no longer towards what would have seemed proper to such nineteenth- and early twentieth-century figures as Mazzini, Kossuth or Woodrow Wilson, i.e., towards 'national self-determination', the process of separating out 'nations' with a common linguistic and cultural heritage, and giving them separate states in which to operate. To an overwhelming degree, it has been towards the conversion of administrative units in European overseas empires into sovereign states, whether these units' populations comprised recognisable 'nations' or not. Throughout Africa, Asia, the Middle East and the Caribbean the process has continued, so as to provide the 150 members of the United Nations. (There were 60 members of the League of Nations at its apogee.) This particular movement has been so strong that we are now less likely to use the terms 'nation' and 'national state' to describe a sovereign state than thirty or forty years ago, although we still use 'nationalism' to describe the assertion of so-called 'national interests' by a particular state.[2] It would be hard to call Nigeria or Malaysia a 'nation' in the way that we can still use the term for Japan or France; but Nigeria and Malaysia are both effective states. They stand or fall, not by reason of linguistic or cultural unity, but on account of the degree of unity derived by their peoples from the services which the states provide.

To put the matter in this way is to raise the question: why do sovereign states continue to proliferate? If there is anything at all in the criticisms outlined earlier, why do peoples not seek other forms of political unit? What is there about the sovereign state which enables it, not only to survive, but to reproduce itself in what are often unpromising circumstances?

II

To answer these questions, we must ask what states actually do for (and to) their citizens, and what response those citizens display; this means asking what the notion of loyalty amounts to in the context of the contemporary state. It is perhaps wise, however, to say something first about the variety of sovereign states, since the reader is bound to ask whether one can sensibly speak of 'the sovereign state' as 'doing' this or that, when states vary so greatly in size, resources and social organisation. China is not like Nauru; Singapore has little in common with Nigeria. We call each of them a sovereign state, because that is its legal and diplomatic status; but what else do they have in common?

The answer is that they act alike to the extent that the legal status carries with it certain opportunities and obligations; and that, in addition, states learn quickly from one another about the roles they can play and the responses they can hope to evoke from their citizens. In earlier centuries, with poorer communications, states could and did operate in vastly different ways. The fact that there was not much contact between them (e.g., between those of Europe and Asia, or between these and the kingdoms of Africa) meant that they could largely live to themselves. But increasing contact in the last few centuries, along with the growth of European colonialism, meant that states outside Western Europe were increasingly brought within the diplomatic system, which, with its codification at the Congress of Vienna, entailed both rights and duties and certain standards of performance. In this sense, sovereign states are customarily approximated to one another for purposes of formal diplomacy, regardless of their relative size and strength. Some, like Iran in 1980, may break ranks; but this is a rare occurrence.

It is not only within the diplomatic system that some degree of similarity has developed amongst states. Throughout the industrial era, new states have tended to choose European and American models for their institutions, and have sought to acquire technology from the same sources. Those efforts can be seen today in the determination of new states to have their own airlines, in their attempts to provide education services similar to those of richer and older states, in their elaborate provision (often building upon colonial foundations, as elsewhere) for health and administrative services and in their desire to achieve the budgetary and statistical standards of older states with much more developed economies. The same urge is also present, of course, in the troubled attempts at economic growth of new states. Such processes, observable a century ago in Japan and Thailand, and even earlier in the states of Latin America, are now universal. They provide increasing reason for treating states as if they had much in common, regardless of the differences in their wealth and power.

What this means is that, in contrast with the relative uniqueness characteristic of Chaka's Zulu kingdom, or the Khmer empire, or the administrations of the Bey of Tunis and the king of Dahomey, their present-day successors roughly approximate to one another and to more highly-developed states in the things that they do. These can be broadly grouped under the headings of coercion, representation, provision and mobilisation.

Coercion is the simplest and clearest aspect of the sovereign state, and has sometimes been taken as its dominant characteristic. Engels saw the development of the state in three aspects: its territorial definition, the appearance of public force (i.e., armies, prisons, police forces) and the imposition of taxes.[3] Of these, the two effective aspects embody coercion. The state's coercive power is exercised internally, in keeping law and order, punishing criminals, taxing the citizens, conscripting people into military service and other like activities; it is exercised externally by levying tariffs and other restrictions on the free flow of people, goods and money, and in making war. Coercion may involve both advantage and disadvantage for the citizens of the state, e.g., those who pay taxes internally may be compensated, as it were, by having their jobs and businesses made safe by tariffs. In a sense, coercion remains the basis of the implied social contract between any state and its citizens; they obey it in return for what they get out of it — though their degree of obedience, as measured by tax evasion and similar activities, is rarely absolute.

Representation is my way of categorising those activities of the state which emphasise the so-called national identity of the country and remind the citizen of his place in it — together with those which register his needs and interests, bringing them to the notice of the authorities who are in a position to gratify them. Representation is achieved through national symbols, through the political process embodied in parliaments and the like, and also through the diplomatic system. To what extent the state provides a clarification and expression of personal identity is a moot point. No doubt there are people in all countries to whom Bosanquet's notion of the state is appropriate:

> The State . . . is to the general life of the individual much as . . . the family with regard to certain of his impulses. The idea is that in it, or by its help, we find at once discipline and expansion, the trans-figuration of partial impulses, and something to do and to care for,

such as the nature of a human self demands. If, that is to say, you start with a human being as he is in fact, and try to devise what will furnish him with an outlet and a stable purpose capable of doing justice to his capacities — a satisfying object of life — you will be driven on by the necessity of the facts at least as far as the State, and perhaps further.[4]

This sense of exaltation in the presence of the state is rarely expressed in such explicit terms, but it may well be part of many people's notion of what being a citizen entails. At all events, states universally cultivate the idea that they truly represent their citizens, and that their conduct is governed by those citizens' wishes.

Provision is the most obvious and significant aspect of the state's relations with its citizens, and continually increases in importance. Internally, budgets are largely devoted to providing for particular interests. In developed countries, this process extends to elaborate systems of pensions, health care and the like; to assistance to farmers and ailing manufacturers; to education in its various forms; and, above all, to the maintenance of the governmental structure, with its opportunities for officials, politicians and soldiers. Much the same pattern is evident in underdeveloped countries, except that usually their economies are unable to support elaborate systems of social services and rural assistance, or of education; it is noticeable, however, that provision is made for large-scale governmental structures with much the same beneficiaries as in developed countries.

Such direct assistance from budgets to individuals and organised groups is paralleled by provision for investment (roads, airports, harbour works, hospitals, schools, etc.) in particular regions of the country, so that the state can be identified as benefactor to those areas. It can be identified in the same way through its policies of discrimination against foreigners (through tariffs, quotas, bounties, controls on investment, immigration, etc.), which may be held to benefit particular industries, areas and social groups. Above all, its provision of armed force can be represented as protection of the country as a whole. In many underdeveloped countries, especially in Latin America, the Middle East and Asia, armies are large and military spending is disproportionate. Under such circumstances (as, similarly, with the disproportionate support for farming industries in the USA, Western Europe and Australia) what is represented as the protection of the country as a whole is much more directly the protection of a particular interest.

The more developed a country, the more complex is the network of provision, and the more widespread throughout society is the extension of provision likely to be. The less developed the country, the more likely it is that provision will be largely confined to official, military, professional and business elites. In either case the effect of provision is to bind groups of people more closely to the state, and to the need for its preservation; without it (or, rather, without it in the particular form of regime which benefits them) their source of livelihood would be lost. Provision is the means whereby the representing function of the state obtains its reality of impact.

Mobilisation is what the state tries to do when it reserves to itself the right to mobilise loyalty in national terms by means of flags, anthems, parades, displays of national symbols, awards to individuals and sections and other forms of internal propaganda. Conversely, the state is trying to do the same when it censors criticism by dissidents at home and journalists from abroad, imposes standards of public morality by censoring books and films and insists on controlling television programmes. It may uphold the national language and (if there is one) the national religion, glorify successful sporting performers and otherwise convey the impression that whatever is good in the country is due to action or encouragement by the state.

As already suggested, all of these functions are performed by every state, but they vary in content from one to another, and are performed in a relatively sketchy or sophisticated fashion in accordance with national wealth and the predilections of the rulers and ruled. Their general effect is usually to consolidate the position of the authorities. In carrying out the functions, the existing regime is, to all intents and purposes, the state for the time being. There is, however, a strong continuing element of authority which survives any particular regime; it is compounded of the social characteristics, historical experience and political traditions of the state, and can be recognised as maintaining continuity even after most revolutions. There is more in common between Chinese administrations, before and after the revolution, than between a Chinese revolutionary administration and a Russian revolutionary administration; and vice versa. Whoever captures the commanding heights of a state's administration can usually rely on this element of continuity to bolster his position. It assists mobilisation.

III

Given that states perform the functions which have been described, and that these are what they have in common, however large or small they may be, we may try to answer the further questions about loyalty: Why do people support sovereign states? Why do they seek to create more of them? What opportunities are there for alternative forms?

In part, people support sovereign states because they have to, there being no alternative open to them. If they try to opt out of their responsibilities to obey the law, pay taxes and serve in the wars, they will be fined or put in gaol — unless it seems too much trouble to make martyrs of them. Their chances of emigration are usually slim. They are born into a particular state and stay there; they are bound to it by family, job, property and by ignorance and fear of what it would be like to live somewhere else. In this sense, the country in which one lives can hope to generate loyalty, based upon attachment, whether it is effectively unified 'nationally' (i.e., in terms of language and culture), or whether it is multilingual and multicultural and has alien rulers. Patriotism is, indeed, much older than our notions of the modern state or the nation state. Dr Johnson found a place for it in his *Dictionary*, describing a patriot as 'one whose ruling passion is the love of his country'; his other, more famous, definition of patriotism as 'the last refuge of a scoundrel' was meant, according to Boswell, to mean not 'a real and generous love of our country, but that pretend patriotism which so many, in all ages and countries, have made a cloak for self interest'.[5] Johnson did not include a definition of 'nationalism' in his *Dictionary*, and the Oxford dictionary does not trace it back beyond 1844, though it is prepared to accept 'nationalist' from 1715.

The point of this apparently irrelevant disquisition is that one can find adequate explanation for loyalty to the state by going no further than attachment to the territory which the state controls. Especially in war, as the German and Russian examples showed in World War II, the defence of the land is the strongest of reasons for supporting the most tyrannical of regimes. Englishmen in the Middle Ages were happy to celebrate the victories of Crecy and Poitiers, in spite of their having been won in the name of a king more French than English.

A second, closely linked situation is that in which the land acquires a double measure of patriotism; not only is it where one lives, but the others who live there speak the same language and are recognisably the same sort of people. The number of states to which this condition applies is an increasingly smaller proportion of the total, with France and Spain badgered by dissident Corsicans and Basques, but continuing to be notable examples, as are Greece and Finland. Japan, however, is probably the most unified of the states which can claim ethnic and linguistic nationalism as their prime characteristic.

As we have noted, this nineteenth- and early-twentieth-century basis for the state is no longer the main one. No one would deny that ethnic, cultural and linguistic bonds can provide a strong basis for loyalty, but most modern states contain sizeable minorities which do not share these bonds with the majority. There are other states in which no particular group can be identified as an undisputed majority. The only bonds which keep such states together are those of the language and the network of governmental activities left behind by colonial powers. The network is utilised and extended by the rulers of the new state for purposes of coercion, representation, provision and mobilisation.

This third situation provides a basis for loyalty which depends not upon appeals to tradition and a common culture, but upon the services and protection which the state can provide. We can call the resultant, 'state nationalism'. The product of what some states call 'nation-building', it is a form of patriotism in which concern for one's country is combined with concern for the benefits provided by the state. Whether the community is divided into ethnic and linguistic groups or not, the emphasis of the state's propaganda will be on how well the citizens are treated, and how much worse off they would be if neighbouring states could make inroads on them or control them. (In the case of great powers, the emphasis will be on how badly the citizens would be treated if some other great power controlled them, whether it is a neighbour or not; for most peoples, however, neighbours constitute the most easily understood danger.) By stressing the special favours which specific groups get from the state, together with the national symbols which every state attempts to muster, each state can cultivate a sort of nationalism; and from this it can expect to derive loyalty on a fairly large scale — even, perhaps some of that idealised sentiment which Bosanquet thought only a State could provoke. In this context it does not matter that the population of the state consists of disparate elements. The example of the United States shows that state nationalism can succeed on a vast scale; the promise of American life, the advantages to be gained by citizens, the contrast between conditions in the countries of their ethnic origin and the opportunities of the new state, have been sufficient to generate a high degree of patriotism.

The essence of the American example has been protection and opportunity, though physical provision has bulked much larger than the critics of the USA are usually prepared to admit. It would be difficult to convince the majority of Americans that they needed some alternative to the sovereign state, provided the sovereign state was the one in which they live. Much the same is true in countries of less opportunity. There are some — notably the Soviet Union — which find it necessary to coerce people into staying and not emigrating, but these are exceptions. Most states have no problem in retaining their people in the mass, though there may be dissatisfied sections of the elite — as in India — who see their futures elsewhere, and whose emigration is held up, not by their own governments, but by those of other countries to which they wish to go.

Powerful charges can be levelled against the sovereign state as an institution; but these, as stated earlier in this essay, are essentially of a highly generalised, even abstract character, and as such unlikely to affect individual citizens. It is the world which is normally said to be worse off because of the activities of sovereign states, not their citizens, whether viewed as individuals or as competing interests. Even where it is argued that protectionist and militarist policies adversely affect the people of the state which puts them into effect, this is very much an attitude *sub specie eternitatis;* it does not touch the immediate concerns of the citizen at the time at which the policies are applied, so much as afterwards, when he may be in no position to blame (or even identify) the policies which led to his condition. The situation of the sovereign state is rather like that of the family, which is subject to the strongest criticisms, but continues to reproduce itself. Both are human forms which suit people. They may not suit everyone, but they suffice for most. The advantages are obvious; the disadvantages are either over-intellectualised in formulation, or occur on such a scale as to make no immediate impact on most people's awareness. The state provides and protects; there is no obvious alternative to it. Schemes for integration of states are most likely to succeed when they approximate to the functions of a new sovereign state in which all existing interests will be safeguarded at the expense of foreigners.

IV

If we assume that sovereign states will continue to exist as the basic units of international relations, how is the international system likely to be affected? In answering this question, it is desirable to divide one's attention so as to concentrate in succession on two significant character-istics of states as we know them: their formal equality, and their manifest inequality of size, resources and strength.

Formal equality, the diplomatic basis on which the system of sovereign states has successfully maintained itself for some centuries, implies that there will not be, in anything like the foreseeable future, a world government. The kinds of things which states do could not be done by a world government without the risk that certain states or groups of states would suffer in the provision of scarce resources. The whole notion of protection — whether in physical or economic terms — which is fundamental to the present operation of the sovereign state would be placed in jeopardy. It is impossible to imagine the governments and citizens of existing states deliberately placing themselves in the position of mendicant provinces in a world governed by others of greater size and strength, or placed in a strategically advantageous position.

One does not need to peer ahead to the possible challenge of a proposal for world government in order to see continuing consequences of the preservation of formal equality amongst 150 states or more. General international agreements are becoming harder to conclude (though we should recognise that they have never been easy). The more states there are, the more diverse are the interests to be reconciled, and the more significant are the temporary coalitions which can be formed in order to gain a majority for a particular policy, or to prevent one from being adopted. The proliferation of interests in respect of the law of the sea is a case in point; so are the abortive conferences held on aspects of the proposed New International Economic Order (NIEO).

A further consequence is the expanding separation between great-power politics and the politics of comprehensive international bodies such as the United Nations. The League of Nations was a highly Eurocentric body, yet the European powers of the interwar period preferred to conduct their vital discussions in private, for example at Locarno or Munich, rather than at Geneva. The United States and the Soviet Union have long been accustomed to even greater privacy for their vital talks; they use the UN as a propaganda machine to be pointed by one against the other, but they conduct no significant negotiations within its confines. The UN and its specialised agencies, for their part, have become increasingly the vehicle of pressure and propaganda by small, weak states. We can expect the General Assembly to continue along this path, because of the emphasis placed on formal equality by the UN Charter. The Security Council, which did not originally have this emphasis, but has come to acquire it in practice, will continue to be something of a meeting-ground between great, medium and small powers, but will be largely a registration point for agreements arrived at elsewhere.

In economic terms, the persistence of a system of formally equal sovereign states is likely to make the protectionist principle more respectable than it is now. In the 1950s and 60s, an expanding world economy, together with the zeal of US administrations for freer trade, confirmed the view of orthodox Western economists that all states would benefit from a reduction of trade barriers — though it was recognised that some underdeveloped countries might, under carefully defined circumstances, need to protect their infant industries. Such Millite orthodoxy, characteristic of periods of expanding international trade, made much less sense in the 1970s, when lower rates of economic growth and increasing unemployment in the developed countries led to demands for more protection against imported goods. This protectionism, linked with demands for more effective internal economic management, showed that the classical economic vision of a free flow of resources and optimum division of labour had become as unattainable abroad, for most countries, as it was at home.

At the same time there was a concerted demand from newly industrialised countries such as Korea that they be given easier access to the markets of developed countries; but this demand was matched by the wish of other underdeveloped countries to restrict their home markets to the products of their own industries, or to place restrictions on the activities of the multinational corporations which might be the vehicle of their industrialisation to the point at which they could echo Korea. No doubt the demand for better access to the markets of the developed countries will continue to be heard from newly industrialised countries (notably in East Asia); but this will be no substitute for protective policies for those less favoured in the eyes of international investors, and lacking the same devotion and skill on the part of their workforces as displayed for the time being by the Koreas and Taiwans.

These likely results of formal equality between states are essentially continuations of the existing situation, in which the impact of so many new states has been felt for some time. More interesting results, perhaps, will flow from the essential inequality of states, that which is actual and felt by them when they attempt to push their formally equal status further than their strength will allow. However we view these results, they will be a mixture; it would be simple-minded in the extreme to assume that stronger states will invariably be able to do what they like with smaller ones, subject to some tempering of their power by obeisance to the notion of formal equality. There has never been a time when great powers constantly ran roughshod over lesser powers, though the Forty Years War and the Napoleonic Wars would seem to approximate such periods. It has more often been the case that some great powers have run roughshod over some smaller ones, in accordance with what they felt to be their immediate interests.

This kind of behaviour has become rarer since World War II. There have been notable examples (Britain and France over Suez in 1956 —

though this was hardly a robust case; the USA in Central America and the Caribbean — though these cases were fragmentary and irresolute, compared with American actions in the same area in former times; and, at the time of writing, the USSR in Afghanistan — though this may not be a wholehearted expression of Soviet wishes, but a short-term operation comparable with the Finnish episode of 1939-40). What is more notable, however, is the absence of more examples. It has become harder for great powers to operate as they would have done in earlier times, partly because of the possibility of touching off nuclear warfare, but mainly because of the power of the weak to resist — resulting in uproar at the UN and elsewhere, and endless explanations which have to be made to Third-World states.

It has clearly become more advantageous for great powers to operate indirectly and over the long term when they wish to influence smaller ones, and only in desperation or confusion to attempt to use force. Indeed, it seems possible that the use of force by great powers against small will decline in favour of economic and diplomatic pressures, and that great powers will regard the obloquy resulting from the use of force as not worth incurring, except where they consider that vital interests are affected.

This does not mean, of course, that great powers will give up their attempts to influence smaller ones, or will confine their use of pressure to situations in which crises may develop. It is much more likely that great powers will attempt to consolidate, wherever possible, those spheres of influence which have been a fairly constant feature of their operations in past times. The essentially dependent nature of many small states (e.g., those of former French colonies in Africa upon France, those of the Caribbean upon the United States) leads naturally to sphere of influence arrangements. In other cases, the mere proximity of a great power may create such a situation (e.g., the possibility of China's securing such a sphere of influence in Southeast Asia), unless some other great power or superpower seeks to block it (e.g., the ambiguous situation of the USSR in respect of the Middle East, and the attempts of the USA over many years to prevent the extension of its influence).

A sphere of influence may be operated in more than one way. While we think of it as essentially a case of one great power saying 'keep out' to other great powers in respect of a given area, there are at least three ways in which the practice of a 'closed door' policy may be effected. It can range from 'the door open only to me', to 'the door may be open to others but will certainly be open to me', and on to 'me as the door keeper'.[6] Which will be chosen by a particular great power in a particular area is very much a function of the connections between the politics of the area and the politics of the world as a whole. Here we are confronted with political situations in which the quest for 'the authorities' is the essential task of analysis; but the factor of time is also of major significance, since no sphere of influence lasts for ever, and quickening changes in world politics may suddenly curtail or alter the operation.

Just as the inequality of states in a diplomatic system assuming formal equality may lead to spheres of influence rather than conquests, so it may lead, in other cases, to more attempts at international commodity cartels or pressure-groups composed of states (such as OPEC) and to attempts at regional organisations (such as ASEAN, the Nordic Council, and the South Pacific Forum). These we can view as responses by smaller states to the opportunities provided by their statehood, and to the fear of a 'divide and rule' policy on the part of great powers. On the one hand the small states have acquired the right to band together, and to present the outcome as a *fait accompli* which great powers are called upon to accept; on the other they are necessarily aware that little can be done by either cartels or regional bodies unless there is persistent support from the members, and at least the chance of benevolent acceptance by some larger power or powers. Both sorts of body are liable to decay from within and destruction — genteel, perhaps, but destruction none the less — from without. Neither supply nor demand is assured for any commodity.

Regionalism is a more alluring prospect for many smaller states than cartelisation, since most of them have no commodity which approximates to oil and can be cartelised in the OPEC manner. Yet regionalism may often prove a will-o'-the-wisp. It has made little headway in Latin America, in spite of strenuous efforts over a long period. It is a forlorn hope in the Indian subcontinent. It is a bad joke in the Middle East. Its failure to make headway in these instances is often blamed on the stubbornness of national leaders and the existence of local fantasies and shibboleths; but a more effective political explanation would be that the states of these areas operate in such different ways with such different aims, and are often so much in active competition, that the advantages of regionalism simply do not apply to them in sufficient measure to make it a suitable choice. Because Western Europe is a manageable region, it does not follow that others are.

V

The outcome of a persistence of sovereign states in the international system is not difficult to foresee in broad terms. The system will not be especially different from that which we now have. The obvious features of the present system, of which superpower conflict between the USA and the USSR is the most notable, will continue; so will the determination of second-rank powers such as France, Germany and Japan to retain their high standards of living and their international influence. All of these powers will, however, pay more attention to Third-World countries and to those third-rank powers (the Belgiums, Swedens and Australias on the one hand, and the Brazils, Indias and Nigerias on the other) which represent opportunities for economic gain.

It will be especially necessary for major powers to take account of Third-World opinion on matters which directly affect Third-World states, and which may complicate relations between the major powers themselves. The course of events in regard to Rhodesia (later Zimbabwe) is an instructive example. When Rhodesia made its unilateral declaration of independence in 1965, the matter was regarded as very much one for Britain to solve within the context of the Commonwealth of Nations: Rhodesia was a British dependency; other former British dependencies interested in its future, such as Zambia and Tanzania, were members of the Commonwealth; South Africa, a significant element in the situation, was in close but not intimate relations with Britain. The Organisation of African Unity and the African states at the UN agreed that the matter should be left in the Commonwealth sphere, where African members would do their best to persuade the British government to use force against the Smith regime in Rhodesia. In the event, this effort was a failure, and Rhodesia went its own way. However, when Portugal suffered a change of regime a decade later, and its colonies near to Rhodesia became sovereign states, the matter was taken up again, this time with the active encouragement of the United States. US policy-makers were concerned lest the new, vaguely Marxist, successor states in Angola and Mozambique should become Russian satellites in Southern Africa; at the same time, they recognised that the vaguely pro-Western regimes in Zambia, Tanzania and Botswana might be driven towards a pro-Russian position if the white regime in Rhodesia remained as a running sore. The upshot was intense diplomatic activity, with Britain brought back into a position of apparent authority through US pressure and the fitful support of Commonwealth states. Pressure was also brought to bear on South Africa to agree to a black majority in the Rhodesian parliament. The whole situation had been transformed from the relatively simple one of 1965; issues within Rhodesia remained basically the same, but the existence around Rhodesia of so many sovereign black states, potentially of such importance to the United States, Britain and South Africa, required a wider and more intense international treatment.

As a not dissimilar case, one could take the careful treatment of Iran by the US government during the 'hostages' crisis in 1979-80 and contrast it with the summary treatment received from the US government through the CIA when Iran nationalised the Anglo-Iranian Oil Company in 1951. In both cases, a great power had to act more effectively, more circumspectly and on a much wider scale when dealing with a disturbance affecting the new states.

If we revert to the framework of analysis described in Essay 1, we can see that the world of states consists of inequality, interests and government, as suggested there, but that 'government' is very much a shifting concept which is perhaps better called 'authority'. States are the main interests within the international system. Authority is exercised, now by superpowers, now by individual great powers, now by a complex of opinion and pressure representing the newer, poorer states; but in each situation which we encounter, we should be able to give 'authority' a concrete existence. There is no sign that states will disappear; the tendency is towards more of them.

Having made this point, it needs to be modified if we are to remain founded in reality. The prominence given to sovereign states in this essay, and throughout this book, does not mean that sovereign states constitute the only form of interest in international politics, however much it may indicate that they are the main interests. Nor does it mean that formal equality gives each of them the right to be regarded as having the same significance as every other. Their situation is rather like that of citizens in a community; each has a vote, but the power which can be put behind the vote varies in accordance with wealth and strength. Some states matter much more than others, and there are non-state actors in the international system (such as multinational corporations, churches, branches of Islam) which may, in certain circumstances, also matter more.

At this point we can see that, whether states differ in strength or not and are sometimes outweighed by other international interests, their unique status gives them the opportunity to exist and to exert pressure, even in cases where rational inquiry might suggest, from *a priori* reasoning, that no state should exist at all. The functions which states (even the smallest) perform enable them to continue in being, and to take their place in the principal game which states play, that of diplomacy — to which we now turn.

Notes

1. Notably in F.H. Hinsley, *Sovereignty* (London, 1966).

2. The best recent treatment of the problem of what constitutes a 'nation' and what we mean by 'nationalism' in concrete terms is in Hugh Seton-Watson, *Nations and States* (London, 1977).

3. F. Engels, *The Origin of the Family, Private Property and the State,* ch. IX.

4. Bernard Bosanquet, *The Philosophical Theory of the State* (London, 1910), p. 150. Bosanquet's State was a highly idealised one, but so is the state which many patriots and adherents of particular regimes postulate. The idealising tendency is always present in politics. It is only fair to point out that Bosanquet's State went beyond the apparatus of government, to embrace other aspects of social life; at the same time, he gave a special significance to the State's use of force, as a means whereby the citizens exercised a superior form of self-discipline.

5. James Boswell, *Life of Samuel Johnson,* entry for 7 April 1775. The reference to the *Dictionary,* and to the lack of 'nationalism' is from R.B. Mowat, *International Relations* (London, 1931), p. 1.

6. I am indebted to Professor H. Bradford Westerfield of Yale University for these crisp statements.

Diplomacy, in the classic words of Sir Ernest Satow,

> is the application of intelligence and tact to the conduct of official relations between the governments of independent states, extending sometimes also to their relations with vassal states; or, more briefly still, the conduct of business between states by peaceful means.[1]

It includes not only diplomatic representation in the narrow sense, but the conduct of international conferences, summit meetings, commercial agreements, international organisations and aid agreements; increasingly, as states sponsor and direct activities which previously were left to private bodies, such as sport and scholarship, it includes consideration of these too. In all these spheres, no matter how much they expand in number and quantity, the qualities of good diplomacy remain very much as they were; so much so that Sir Nevile Bland, in revising Satow's work in 1956, was able to retain the long section which Satow had quoted from Callières' *De la manière de negocier avec les souverains* on the qualities of the good negotiator. This was originally published in 1716.

I

What has happened is that, although the concerns of the modern state are so much wider than those of the sovereigns of the eighteenth century, and the machinery of communication is so much more intricate and immediate, a state's demands are still presented as those of a sovereign body which, potentially at any rate, is prepared to use sanctions in pursuit of what it wants. The sovereign state, as we have seen, has been enhanced in its role as protector of its people's interests and mouthpiece of their wishes. The growth of international trade and investment, whether in the conventional form or in its more contemporary form as economic aid, has made the state more, not less, important to its citizens. It acts as their shield and representative; it protests when terms are bad, seizes chances when they are good, moves to supplement international arrangements when these do not seem to suit private ends. When it enters into international commitments, whether economic, military or otherwise, it does so against a background of domestic interests of which the dominant ones must be satisfied if the commitment is to be a success.

The ancient task of a country's diplomacy in protecting its citizens is given new meaning by each fresh complexity introduced into the international system. The state becomes stronger, not weaker; government has more to do; the tasks of representation become more complex. Yet they are, in essence, the same tasks. Diplomacy helps to ameliorate conflict by registering one state's interests in the capital of another which might possibly place them in jeopardy. A diplomat must still do the best he can for his country without getting it into more trouble than it would be in if he did nothing. He must still deal with official representatives of other countries, and occasionally with private ones. The techniques he employs — to be cautious without being offensive, to be forceful without being rude, to be prudent without shutting off all information, to be tactful without actually telling lies, to be always aware of the broad range of his country's interests, to be observant without being indicted as a spy, to make concessions without seeming weak and grasp opportunities without showing undue satisfaction — these are as applicable to an agreement about chicken exports from the United States to the European Economic Community, or wheat exports from Australia to China, as to anything done in former times at the Porte or the Quai d'Orsay. The unfortunate Mr Mills, in David Footman's novel of consular life, *Pig and Pepper*,[2] may have felt that the Department of Overseas Trade was wasting its time when it sent him, in dusty Tsernigrad, an elaborate questionnaire concerning possible outlets for British toothbrushes. No one seemed to use them, and they were always put on the list of prohibited luxury imports when the local Minister of Finance wished to show how keenly he was acting to restore the balance of trade. But Mr Mills's situation was simply epitomising, at the extreme of absurdity, the pressure upon the modern state to satisfy its people's demands on the outside world, and the strain put upon its representatives. No matter what groupings states find themselves in the task of diplomacy is to ensure that the interests of the particular state are not ignored or affronted.

I am not suggesting that the life of states is that war of all against all which we associate with Hobbes's picture of unregulated mankind, or, rather, I am not suggesting that it is like that all the time. We see too much evidence of cooperation between states to think that war is the proper description of how they live together. Yet we cannot ignore the potentialities of acrimony, of discrimination, and, in the last resort, of violence. If Albania can be found in bitter arguments with two great communist states which were assumed to dominate it; if Cuba, by a change of regime, can become the principal opponent of the United States in the American hemisphere; if India and Pakistan, so alike in so many things, can be permanently at odds; if African states can quarrel so bitterly — then we are entitled to think of hostility as a potential condition for any states at all, no matter how they might be situated at the moment.

II

It is to the diplomat that states look to convey their interests to one another and to secure what advantages are possible. He, rather than the politician, is the most purely representative figure of our time. Behind him stand his whole country and its aims, as expressed through the machinery of asserting, moderating and reconciling interests which its government employs. He is the point of contact between policy and the world outside. His personal views may be considered by his government, but must, in action, be set aside in favour of theirs. He must take upon himself the full import of his government's wishes, no matter how distasteful they may be to him at times. Thus he has, forced upon him, a particular non-moral role which may be hard or easy to play, depending upon his conscience but may seem to the critical onlooker at times a despicable one. The diplomat's is a genuine political dilemma. He is satisfied that his country must be represented; otherwise he would not be representing it. He is, of necessity, a special kind of patriot whose loyalty is to the state in the abstract, but who can go against its government of the day only at the risk of resignation or disgrace. In this he is akin to the professional soldier. A change of regime may create insuperable problems for him (though these may be removed by his replacement by someone closer to the new regime); but he is not justified, so long as he retains his diplomatic status, in showing any overt opposition to his governments's policies.

The diplomat's is a genuine political dilemma, but it is not the same for all diplomats at all times. In the traditional democratic countries, a change of regime does not usually mean substantial change in foreign policy. In the countries accustomed to despotism or one-party rule, a change of faces at the top may not cause much anxiety in a diplomatic post. The most difficult problems arise for the representatives of states normally free and constitutional, who find that their government has changed to one of naked power exercised in different interests from those to which they were accustomed. German diplomats in the 1930s are the archetypes of the diplomat's possible dilemma.

Diplomacy is thus, in spite of its essentially political and representative character, a highly personal affair. The diplomat may be such a booby as Evelyn Waugh's Sir Samson Courtenay, who found an inflated india-rubber sea-serpent in the bathroom and sat in the warm water engrossed in it; 'chance treats of this kind made or marred the happiness of this Envoy's day.'[3] He may lack the combined ingenuity and vapidity of Our Man in Havana. He may have to be fished out of trouble by saturnine men from his country's security service, as seems to be increasingly the way in thrillers. He may, on the other hand, be in the position of Sir Arthur Nicolson, who, after concluding the Anglo-Russian Convention of 1907, wrote to his wife, 'How I hate politics, yet how I love them';[4] or like Sir Arthur's son, who wrote in his diary on the signing of the Treaty of Versailles, 'It has all been horrible . . . To bed, sick of life.'[5] The young Harold Nicolson and his fellows in the British delegation were ashamed of the prior commitments of their country to Italy in the secret treaties that brought Italy into the war, and distressed at much of the content of the Treaty signed at Versailles; but they could see no way in which they could speak out. Yet they could not help their feelings.

III

It is inevitable that tension should gather at times between the diplomat's feelings and what he has to say. It is inevitable too that his situation may seem artificial. These are the prices paid for retaining the system as it stands, a system whereby some of the niceties of discourse are retained between states which might be at one another's throats if the simple facts of power between them were translated into action on impulse. The whole apparent nonsense of formal equality between states which are manifestly unequal, of immunity and of seniority, enables small states and big ones, new ones and old, black ones and white, to act as if they were equal partners in joint enterprises, or equal opponents in negotiation. Nothing can finally blunt the edge of naked power, if a government is able and determined to wield it; but the conventions of diplomacy provide a set of basic rules within which negotiation can be carried on even by regimes which dislike one another. Undoubtedly there are all sorts of costs in the system — costs in time and human patience, as well as in money spent on cocktail parties — but they help to retain it in a relatively civil condition. It is worth emphasising that Satow's brief definition of diplomacy was, 'the conduct of business between states *by peaceful means*'. (My emphasis.) When negotiation disappears, and brute force controls, there is much less room for diplomacy. But only a few men, at any time in history, want to conduct international relations by brute force if it can possibly be helped.

It is sometimes suggested that the diplomat's role is different now from what it was under the 'old diplomacy', the state of affairs which is assumed to have come to an end in 1914 or 1919. Nuclear horrors are said to have rendered diplomacy futile; popular demand, substituted for the conversation of aristocrats, is said to have displaced negotiation. This is a typical journalistic exaggeration. It is true that there are now many areas of what is sometimes called 'fringe diplomacy', involving economic officials, information officers and a host of special experts; diplomatic staff may sometimes be submerged by the rising tide of these, and their contacts may be with officials in departments other than Foreign Offices, so spoiling the notion of diplomacy as being essentially a discussion between Foreign Offices. Nevertheless, this does not make a great difference. It does, of course, call for a higher degree of coordination between different kinds of representation than may have been needed in the past; but in essence it is simply an extension of the system of having naval and military attachés and commercial representatives.

In Harold Nicolson's life of his father, which we may take as an example of the old diplomacy (the elder Nicolson was head of the British Foreign Office after a lifetime in the Diplomatic Service), one is struck by the similarity of many of the situations faced by Nicolson to those facing diplomatists now. His service in Turkey and Morocco in the 1890s and 1900s presented him with many of the same problems as now face diplomats in a number of Asian and African countries — of trying to get his way with local governments, backward and often corrupt, against the competition of other interested powers. The tangle over Turkish railways in 1893, for example, is very like that over aid in, say, Afghanistan in recent times.[6] The Macedonian question in the 1900s, centring in practice round the provision of an international *gendarmerie* from some outside source or sources acceptable to the great powers, is a startling parallel with such situations as those which have occurred in the Congo and the Middle East.[7]

When M. Iswolsky and Lord Hardinge consulted at Reval in 1908 about matters concerning both Russia and Britain, the Russian returned under the impression that he had obtained assurances from the British visitors concerning the Straits. But Hardinge and Iswolsky meant different things by 'the Straits'. Hardinge meant that the Straits might be open to anybody; Iswolsky meant that they should be open to Russia alone.[8] Can we be sure that when foreign ministers discuss the matters of today they are not open to similar misunderstandings? Dr Kissinger seems to have encountered some of them.

When we read of Sir Edward Grey in 1908 describing his answers to the Russian ambassador's questions about what Britain would do if Russia were confronted with certain perfectly possible circumstances, it readily reminds us of British and American indecision in our own time, with its unfortunate effects on friend and foe alike. Sir Edward wrote:

> I concluded, as I had begun, by saying that it was not to be expected that a Cabinet would come to a decision on a question of this kind except under the pressure of a crisis. I could not submit such a question to my colleagues unless it became urgent; and it was no good for me to say anything unless I was authorised to do so by them.[9]

It is not simply that the past is rather like the present; one can always suggest this by choosing the right examples, just as one can find examples to show it is quite unlike the present. Rather, the point is that major difficulties in diplomacy are not matters of a particular moment, but are inherent in the existence of a system of sovereign states, and are likely to crop up, and show their effects, no matter what the technology of the age may be. For example, the existence of weak states not completely under the control of any of the strong ones is likely to create competition between the strong: it may be over opportunities for trade or investment, or because the weak state is assumed to be in a strategically important position; it may be in terms of religious or political affiliation; but tension is likely to develop.

The business of diplomacy is not simply a matter of the ambassadors in this or that country. As Satow says:

> When we speak of the 'diplomacy' of a country as skilful or blundering, we do not mean the management of its international affairs by its agents residing abroad, but their direction by the statesman at the head of the department. Many writers and speakers are disposed to put the blame for a weak or unintelligent diplomacy on the agent, but this mistake arises from their ignorance of the organisation of public business.[10]

When Sir Edward Grey showed the kind of hesitancy instanced just now, he was reacting in what is not solely a characteristic British way to suggestions that he should pledge himself to certain action in a hypothetical future situation; he was displaying the natural caution of any government to commit itself in advance to something which may prove injurious to itself. It is very rarely that governments insist that they will go to war in particular circumstances; when they do, as with the British declaration over Poland in 1939 or the American statements over Cuba in 1962, it is usually a case of recognition in advance of what would otherwise be a *fait accompli*. War is likely to break out in any case, so one might as well be prepared for it and strike, if not the first blow, a resounding second one. No amount of assurance about the capacity of his nuclear weapons is going to remove the hesitancy of a head of government who is asked to say in advance just how far he is prepared to go if things take a particular turn. No matter how ingenious the hypotheses about first or second strikes, capability and credibility, zero-sum or non-zero-sum games, the politician will still have to decide in terms of the support he can get from his party and his people, the likely consequences of his act and the possibility of alternatives. This particular dilemma is no different in kind from what it was before 1914 and 1939. And, of course, by far the greatest number of decisions which make up a nation's diplomacy now are not nuclear decisions at all; they are about relations with this or that country or group of countries which may have ultimate repercussions upon the nuclear balance, but are primarily directed towards the problems of the time.

Perhaps it would make the meaning clearer to draw a parallel between the situation between Britain and Russia in 1906 and that which now exists between Australia and Indonesia. Sir Arthur Nicolson was British ambassador in St Petersburg, and most anxious to arrive at some sort of agreement, partly for its own sake (because there were situations, in Persia and elsewhere, in which the two countries' interests clashed directly), and partly because he did not wish Russia to be permanently aligned with Germany against Britain. He described his situation like this:

> I undertook the post with great diffidence and considerable misgivings. Personally I was most anxious to see removed all causes of difference between us and Russia. I considered that many of these differences were caused by simple misunderstanding of each other, and because each country attributed to the other plans and projects which in reality were not entertained . . . I did not know whether I should not find among the majority of Russians the old traditional

feeling of mistrust and dislike of Great Britain. Moreover in England the feeling towards Russia cannot be described as being at all sympathetic . . . In large sections, Russia was regarded as a ruthless and barbarous autocratic state, denying all liberties to her subjects and employing the most cruel methods . . . I mention these currents of feeling in England as indicating that . . . it would be possible that some event might arouse public opinion in England against the continuance of any discussions.[11]

Moreover, the Russian government was neither friendly nor stable. In ruling circles there were widespread feelings that Britain would applaud Imperial Russia's downfall by revolution, and that Britain's ally, France, was atheist, republican and unreliable. There were many highly-placed Russians who considered that an alliance with Germany was eminently desirable. In all these circumstances Nicolson had to proceed with caution. Behind him were restive English liberals who were suspicious of Russia; across the table from him were men who doubted the motives of his own government, and feared being taken in the rear by other palace factions. Between them fell the shadow of Germany, able to make its own approaches to Russia through a variety of means. Nicolson felt that the only way was to stick to particulars, to try to settle points of friction and thereby secure more confidence between the parties. He succeeded in obtaining agreement, under the Anglo-Russian Convention, on a number of disputed matters relating to Persia, Afghanistan and Tibet. In practice, the Convention did not prevent further friction, especially in Persia, and it did not destroy mutual suspicions; but it helped to clarify intentions and led to the *entente* between Britain, France and Russia which caused Russia and Britain to be on the same side in the war in 1914. It did not prevent that war, or the Russian revolution which followed it. Nicolson's diplomacy did, however, secure a number of short-term objectives without hindering policy in the long term, and it cleared some of the atmosphere. It enabled future negotiation to go forward, though it did not ensure that anything done in the future would be free of misunderstanding or entirely in Britain's interests. How could it?

Now let us compare this situation with one today. Australia and Indonesia are fated to be in one another's company, and there are certain matters on which they may disagree. Any Australian minister or diplomat who wishes to improve relations with Indonesia is in something like the same position as Nicolson and the government behind him. Within Australian public opinion, there is considerable doubt about the friendliness and stability of the Indonesian regime; there is suspicion of Indonesian intentions in neighbouring areas; Indonesian actions in Timor have reinforced these longstanding attitudes. Against this, there is a widespread feeling that Australia must learn to live with Indonesia, since the two countries are neighbours. There is probably more admiration of Indonesia in sections of the Australian community than there was of Russia in England in 1906. On the Indonesian side, there is probably more goodwill as a legacy from the past than the Russians felt towards Britain, but this is curtailed by resentment against what is considered the irresponsible approach of the Australian media. Any negotiator for Indonesia in talks with Australia would be as concerned about palace intrigues at home as the Russian negotiators were. Indonesia is incalculable in something like the same way as Russia was in 1906, though one would have to do a good deal of translating from an imperial and aristocratic system to a nationalist and military one to show how. China's shadow falls across the situation as Germany's did in 1906.

Two points can be made about this parallel. First, any Australian representative attempting a task similar to Nicolson's, i.e., a general settlement with Indonesia, would be wise to go about it in much the same way: that is, seeing how delicate the position was, he would look for limited, matter-of-fact issues which seemed possible of settlement; he would not, I think, aim at the broadest public agreement about major objectives, since this would throw both countries into debate and indecision as to what these objectives were. He would look for minor settlements which did not harm either party's dignity or vital interests, as it interpreted them. Second, the Australian government would be in much the same state of doubt and concern as the British government was; just as it was worried about the effect of any agreement upon France, Germany, Austria and Turkey, so the Australian government would have to take account of Indonesia's partners in ASEAN, which had no counterpart in the Russian case. But it would presumably be of the same mind as the British government was, in thinking that something was needed to prevent the situation deteriorating. Thus it too would look for limited results but hope for a general improvement in the climate of relations. Its representative would have to exert tact and caution of the highest order, while convincing the Indonesians of his country's sincerity. Any agreement which resulted would not change the face of the world, nor eliminate the fundamental differences between the two countries as political entities; but it might assist in mutual understanding and in cooperation where that was possible.

In short, the kinds of problems which Australian negotiators would face (and have faced over Timor, refugees from Indochina and relations between Indonesia and Papua New Guinea) are very much like those faced by Nicolson. So, although we need not say that the old diplomacy and the new are precisely the same, we can assert that the same sorts of problems and procedures, the same considerations to be kept in mind, are fundamental to diplomacy, and are likely to recur so long as we have sovereign states.

IV

It might be asked how much this situation is affected by that change to 'popular' diplomacy which, it is sometimes said, is characteristic of the contemporary world. The widespread use of the term 'popular' diplomacy dates from President Wilson's spectacular appearance in Europe in 1919, when it referred to the way in which his approach seemed to reject traditional diplomatic method, and appeal over the heads of governments to their peoples. But this was more potential than actual, even in Wilson's case. In practice, it was with governments that he dealt, and the only popular appeal he made in the end was to his own people; that appeal was rejected.

It may be that diplomacy now has to be carried on with a greater awareness of what democratic assemblies may say and do than sixty years ago; but again the difference is of degree, not of kind. The United States has always conducted much of its diplomacy at the top of its voice. The example was followed by Gladstone in his Midlothian campaigns. Neither the British nor the German government was averse, in the first decade of this century, to a rousing nationalistic speech, when that seemed likely to have a salutary effect in foreign capitals. The situation now is that, while every nation has to have its turn on the hustings at the General Assembly of the United Nations for the benefit of the newspapers at home, the resolutions which are carried are the result of intimate negotiation behind the scenes, within the African or Third-World bloc, for example, and in conclave between the United States and its associates in its own hemisphere and in Europe. New states learn these crafts quickly; they are natural forms of political expression. Diplomacy has always considered that infinite riches can be garnered in a little smoke-filled room, provided the negotiators stick to their promises.

Similarly, the appearance of summit conferences is not new, nor is there any reason to believe that their conduct is essentially different from what went on at the Congress of Berlin, or even the meeting between

Napoleon and Alexander on the raft at Tilsit. When Disraeli said he had brought back peace with honour, he was not in a very different position to President Kennedy or Mr Khrushchev waving the nuclear test-ban treaty. The background of give and take is much the same; the sense of having averted a slide towards war is the same; the sense of justification in popular terms is much the same too.

It is true that the appearance of the communist states has brought something new into diplomacy, or seemed to have done so while the bloc remained monolithic under the pressure of the Soviet Union and the lack of action on the part of China to alter the situation. Now, however, there is something like conventional diplomacy amongst the countries of communist persuasion. This is true even between China and Vietnam, or the Soviet Union and North Korea; and the successive breakdowns of Albanian relations with the Soviet Union and China have made further nonsense of the one-time claim that relations between communist regimes were generically different (because essentially more harmonious) than those between capitalist regimes. There are suspicions, alliances and understandings between communist states, not simply one general understanding. To say this is not to assert that the communist countries have utterly surrendered to the capitalist method of conducting relations between states. But it is surprising how much they talk in terms of the obligations and assumptions of that method — about international law and custom, for example — and how much the conventions of the system are adaptable to the peculiar position in which the communist countries stand.

What, then, is the shape of diplomacy? It is the shape of an actor in a play; not a naturalistic play such as we are accustomed to, but a play in the Greek or Japanese tradition, in which the actors wear masks and strike attitudes. The mask represents the actor's country. His movements are formal yet graceful, their import recognised in advance by the other actors, whose postures in response have a formal quality too. The diplomatist stands in the play as the representative of his country; he moves gracefully because the character of the moves belongs to convention; yet every movement means something, since he carries with him so many interests and concerns, processed and adjusted through the political system of his country, and judged sufficiently important to be put forward by him as the symbol of his state. His shape and aspect are peaceful, and intended to serve peaceful purposes; the mask may bear a smile or a frown, but normally it will be stylised to represent goodwill. The shadow which the actor casts has an uglier shape, however; it stands for the threat of sanctions, of pressures of various kinds, graded to the situation, which may culminate in war. The fact that the shape is stylised and the movements are conventional must not confuse us. It is what the actor stands for that matters. It is what lies behind the shape, collected and embodied in the shape itself, that we need to know about, no matter how absorbing the play may be.

So far ahead as we can see, this situation will prevail. No doubt, the diplomatist has to be seen in the widest sense — not just as the ambassador to this or that country, but as the special emissary (like Dr Kissinger when he organised the breakthrough to communist China), the leader of the delegation to an international conference, the representative at the UN, the meticulous negotiator of a trade treaty and the expert discussing force levels or interest rates. In all these cases, much the same shape of diplomacy may be seen, in terms of techniques and interests.

Notes

1. Sir Ernest Satow, *A Guide to Diplomatic Practice*, 4th edn, ed. Sir Nevile Bland (London, 1957), p. 1.
2. David Footman, *Pig and Pepper*, 2nd edn (London, 1954). This delightful book's hero comes from Leicester, where I spent many happy years. Unfortunately he, like that more familiar figure in Australian fiction, Richard Mahoney, did not like it.
3. Evelyn Waugh, *Black Mischief* (London, 1932), ch. 2.
4. Harold Nicolson, *Lord Carnock* (London, 1930), p. 255.
5. Harold Nicolson, *Peacemaking, 1919* (London, 1933), pp. 370, 371.
6. Nicolson, *Lord Carnock*, pp. 93-4.
7. Ibid., p. 266.
8. Ibid., p. 273n.
9. Ibid., p. 286.
10. Satow, *A Guide to Diplomatic Practice*, p. 4.
11. Nicolson, *Lord Carnock*, pp. 206-7.

4   THE ROOTS OF FOREIGN POLICY

'Foreign policy' is an ambiguous and perhaps misleading term. When someone asks, 'What is the government's foreign policy?', the emphasis is very much on the aims and attitudes which the government professes, upon the public wishes which it is concerned to satisfy and upon the logical consistency of its approach. In such a context, foreign policy is essentially something to be expounded. It is a matter of what the government says, rather than of what it does. Yet what it does is what matters most: the behaviour of the state towards other states will affect them much more than anything said by the government of the state; talk is cheap, but action is real. If we think of foreign policy as the enunciated approach of a government towards the problems of mankind (which, on the whole, is what people look for at elections and on other rhetorical occasions), we shall miss the significance of much that the government is doing.

There is a further element of ambiguity, arising from the implications of the word 'policy'. When we ask for a policy on something, we have in mind a course of action, prudently and sagaciously worked out, and involving above all the notion of purpose. Yet experience of politics at any level shows that much of what is done is not purposeful, but is the result of compromise, accident or habit. It would be strange if the things done to foreigners were full of purpose while those done towards fellow citizens were haphazard. Another objection to the idea that foreign policy is highly purposeful comes from our awareness that political activity is essentially pluralist, with a variety of interests at work in competition and coordination with one another; the outcome is sometimes the triumph of a particular interest's purpose, but more often the resultant of differing pressures. It is unlikely that foreign policy could be the only exception.

Given these ambiguities and objections, there is a case for either omitting or seriously curtailing the use of the term 'foreign policy'. A more descriptive term might be 'external official behaviour', in spite of its clumsiness as language. It throws the stress on to behaviour, which does not either imply or exclude purpose, but includes actions as well as talk. In its reference to official behaviour, it does not say what sort of behaviour that is, but leaves open the question whether it is the kind which is traditionally associated with diplomacy, or takes other forms. This is a matter of some importance, since a distinction has often been drawn between foreign policy on the one hand, and defence, economic and (in more spacious imperial days) colonial policy on the other. Yet, if one is concerned with the place of the state in world politics, it is clear that other states may be just as much affected — perhaps more so — by economic or colonial policy as by those policies concerned with immediately political relationships, as these affect security.

'External official behaviour' is, however, an outlandish term compared with 'foreign policy', besides being longer. In this essay, 'foreign policy' will be used, but in the extended sense described in the preceding paragraph. Whatever the state does abroad is to be regarded as foreign policy, whether it stems from a conventional foreign ministry or not. There will be no assumption that all acts of policy are the result of deliberate, purposeful decision; rather, while it will be assumed that various interests strive to make foreign policy serve their own purposes, room will be left for the habitual, the haphazard and the inconsistent in what a state does.

To put the matter in this way is not to dismiss altogether the notion of purpose in foreign policy. Much of what states try to do externally is animated by purpose, in that it is intended to influence what other states do. Some policies are meant to encourage other states, some to deter them, some to cultivate them in broad terms, some to persuade them into particular activities, some to defy them. In practice, however, the purposes behind such efforts are hampered and altered by the context in which they have to be undertaken. Not only is the state involved in the process of international politics, which includes both opportunities and restrictions; it is also affected in its external behaviour by domestic forces, some of which will approve of the purpose behind a particular policy, while others will disapprove. The roots of foreign policy, in the sense of what animates the external behaviour of a state, are to be found both abroad and at home.

I

It was clear to John Locke that governments did not have the same authority over foreigners as over their own citizens, and that this put foreign policy into a somewhat different category from domestic policy. He divided the business of government into two parts, which he called 'executive' and 'federative'. By the first he meant the ordinary business of government at home, which he distinguished from 'the power of war and peace, leagues and alliances, and all the transactions with all persons and communities without the commonwealth', which, he said, 'may be called federative if any one pleases. So the thing be understood, I am indifferent as to the name.' He thought that, while the federative power was of great importance, it was

> much less capable to be directed by antecedent, standing and positive laws than the executive ... What is to be done in reference to foreigners, depending much upon their actions and the variation of designs and interests, must be left in great part to the prudence of those who have this power committed to them, to be managed by the best of their skill for the advantage of the commonwealth.[1]

Locke went no further in delineating his federative power (which, in his usage, had nothing to do with federations as we know them today), but his reminder of the difference between one's own fellow countrymen and foreigners is apposite, so long as we do not assume that the difference is absolute. Foreigners are not under a particular state's control, whereas local citizens are to a significant degree: they can be taxed and conscripted, fooled and flattered, by their government; but they have the power of rebellion and may overturn that government, despite its claims to sovereign power. The difference lies in the fact that the people of a state are less likely to obstruct their government's wishes than are those of other, more powerful or more distant states.

Other states represent other interests within the international political system. They are not necessarily hostile (it is a myth that all states wish to be at one another's throats), but they are competitive in those spheres in which scarcity and inequality render one state's advantage another's disadvantage. Many are experienced in the diplomatic processes discussed in Essay 3, and have governments which are capable of deciding, within fairly narrow limits, how far they can go in cooperation or confrontation before their vital concerns are jeopardised. Some are new states, lacking diplomatic experience and resources, and sometimes substituting ideology for clearly established interest. Some again are disposed to consider that they have diplomatic positions to uphold, and that others should normally defer when these positions are stated; the superpowers, with their concern for prestige, are very much in this category. In all these instances, a state's foreign policy position is necessarily affected by the attitudes of the states with which it has to deal.

At any given time, it is fairly clear to the government of a particular state that certain other states are friendly, others hostile and others indifferent; and within this range it is also clear that some are important to the first state's concerns, while others appear not to matter. Making this sort of assessment is part of the business of foreign policy as practised by foreign offices. The problem is, however, that nothing in the situation can be guaranteed to stand still. Especially in periods after wars and other violent convulsions, today's enemy may be tomorrow's friend because of changes in the world at large, or in the other state's regime, or in one's own. Not only may one's own regime change markedly, but new constellations of interest may appear within one's own country and amongst one's allies. Objectives which seemed to be fixed may be replaced by new ones.

At any given time, there is recognisably an international political system, and most states have an interest in preserving it, or at least in preserving important aspects of it even if they wish to change their own positions within it; but changes constantly occur, of which some of the most important may prove widely unpredictable. For example, the system was profoundly affected by the Bolshevik revolution in Russia in 1917, and again by the Sino-Soviet split in 1960; but few people anticipated either these events or their consequences.

There are many ways of deciding the nature of an international system. Each of them has something to be said for it in a situation in which the 'system' is not of the kind that has been deliberately designed, but is essentially a summation of interrelated activities at a particular period.[2] Two concepts which I find useful in seeing how the international system relates to the formation of foreign policy for a given state are those of *hierarchy* and *horizon*.

The notion of hierarchy applies when one is looking at the world as a whole and trying to work out where a particular state fits in. Clearly, some states are bigger, stronger, more widespread in their contacts and concerns and more influential than their fellows. This means that, however one defines power, some are more powerful than others. There is usually little difficulty in agreeing in broad terms about how the grading runs. At the top are the two superpowers, which possess 'global reach' in the sense that they can use their nuclear weapons against targets anywhere in the world. They are also large, diverse countries with substantial populations and modern economies; their power of production enables them to influence other countries' economies, and to be free, in the last resort, of dependence on others. Moreover, they exude hostility towards one another's social and economic systems, and are activated in their external behaviour by knowledge, fear and anticipation of how each might prove more influential in the world at large. This combination of circumstances ensures that they have not only the capacity but also the desire to be constantly active within the international system.

Below them comes a group of secondary powers which includes China, France, Japan, West Germany and perhaps Britain. These are marked by substantial economies and, in most cases, significant armed forces. They may or may not possess nuclear weapons, but are not in a position to contemplate using them against one of the superpowers, even to the limited extent that such a possibility exists for the superpowers themselves — although it is clear that China has the potentiality to become a third superpower, and will achieve this status as soon as it can. The secondary powers are of great importance to the superpowers (notably because of their significance in the world economy) and also to those which stand below them in the hierarchy (for much the same reason, although there may also be other reasons, such as concern about the possibility of future Chinese imperialism, and attachment to France as a former colonial power).

As a third grade in the hierarchy one can distinguish certain large countries which have considerable potential for economic development (such as Brazil, Argentina, India and Nigeria), and smaller countries which have attained standards of production and income comparable to those of the higher grades (examples are Sweden, Switzerland, Australia, Canada, South Africa and, in due course, Korea). These may possess importance because of economic potential, effective economic management, strategic location and the like.

Below these three grades there is the vast array of underdeveloped countries, many of which are either too small or too poor to have much chance of economic growth in the foreseeable future. Economic capacity is not, however, the only criterion by which their relative importance can be assessed. It depends on who is doing the assessment and what interests are involved. Small states which have rich deposits of raw materials, or lie at the entrances of much-used waterways, or are located on or near the borders of superpowers and their close associates, obviously possess importance to a wide variety of more significant states.

One can extend the hierarchy indefinitely, by utilising this or that criterion, but the general significance of the gradings is clear. They do not indicate that any state can coerce another on a lower grade; they simply show that those on the higher grades have widespread importance in the system at large. The fact that the largest number of states is to be found in grades three and four means that these may, through combination and the use of suitable political resources (e.g., the General

Assembly of the United Nations, and the specialised agencies), put pressure upon those further up in the hierarchy. The placing of a particular state in a particular grade does not mean that it will stay there (e.g., China may become a superpower, Brazil or Iran a secondary power, and countries may emerge from the ruck of the underdeveloped to positions of much greater significance). The hierarchy is, as it were, a snapshot of the situation at any given time; it has elements of long-term stability, but is subject to continual change. What it mainly expresses is the range of interest and influence of one state in comparison with another.

The notion of horizon is more figurative than that of hierarchy, being a means of converting the demonstrable hierarchy of states into something more applicable to the interests of a particular state. If we imagine this state as relatively small, relatively new and relatively distant from the epicentre of international activity, the image may become clearer. We can think of the foreign policy-makers of this state as looking out at the world and trying to decide which other countries matter to it. A series of horizons can be imagined. The first and nearest is that of neighbouring states, whether these are small or great. Neighbours have traditionally been important to any state, because of the high incidence of communication with them through trade and travel; the possibility of quarrels over disputed borders; the problem of what kinds of restrictions are needed in order to ensure that neighbours do not gain too much advantage from one's own situation; the effects of having similar or divergent ethnic stock; and so on. In a sense, neighbouring states always matter, even though they may not matter most.

A further horizon is that of major states with which one's own state may have trading, investment, migration, cultural and other connections. This is especially so in the case of former colonial territories, to which the former metropolitan power may, for a time at least, crowd out most other international contacts, and constitute the only visible horizon. France has been more active than Britain in this regard; but in all instances there may be a lingering connection for far longer than it takes for the former colony to assume a sophisticated approach to foreign policy. Such a connection can be seen in the contemporary relations between Portugal and Brazil, and between Spain and the other Latin-American states. A former colonial power, having provided an initial entry into the modern industrial world for its colonies, remains a familiar associate which continues to attract favourable and unfavourable attention. It would be wrong, however, to think of this particular horizon as normally occupied by only the one power. In the case of European colonial powers, which were the main sources of colonial control, a former colony may be led on from Britain to Germany, or France to Italy, in making connections of importance.

A third horizon, which complicates life for all states and especially the newer ones, is that of the superpowers. Since these have global reach, and extend their strategic vision to every part of the world, no state is beyond their interest. They offer economic aid, military aid and help of various kinds; in return they may want loyalty and bases. It is a matter of concern for every state to decide what attitude it will take towards the two super-powers, and whether one is to be preferred to the other without inviting trouble.

There is another horizon which, for want of a more inclusive term, I shall call the horizon of kindred states. In some instances this horizon is clearly defined, although it is still liable to disturbance. Communist states and Muslim states have, as it were, ready-made horizons which by definition are important to them. But, as in the other cases, the notion of a horizon does not establish the policy which a particular state should or will pursue; it simply indicates that a certain group of states will be of importance. Amongst both communist and Muslim states there has been ample room for disagreement and bitter conflict as well as for basic agreement. Most new states do not fit into either of these categories. They have found their horizons of kindred states either in regional connections or in the non-aligned group with its correlated activity within the United Nations system. Thus, African states have, as it were, a continuous horizon which extends through regional connections within Africa, to the Organisation of African Unity, and on to the campaigns at the UN against South Africa and in favour of the NIEO. Industrialised non-communist states have a horizon of kindred states in OECD.

Horizons are helpful if one is trying to adjust a given state's situation to that hierarchy of power which is the general basis for the operation of the international political system. Each state will have a different set of horizons. Superpowers have a global horizon; secondary and tertiary powers have mainly a regional horizon; and the rest tend to have an immediate or neighbourhood horizon. It is important, in any estimation of how a particular state's foreign policy is likely to develop, not to assume that the world looks the same to all states, or that what is significant to one's own state is significant to all. There is a kind of ethno-centrism which affects analysts in superpowers in particular, but is likely to be found anywhere; it consists of assuming that what matters to one's own country must matter to everyone else. This is the very negation of reality in the world of states.

II

Although there is no difficulty in accepting that many of the roots of
foreign policy lie in the behaviour of foreigners and in deciding what to
do about them, there may be more resistance to the idea that those roots
are also to be found in one's own state, and that they may be contradictory
in character, in the sense that there is no single straightforward taproot
growing out of the agreed interests of the country, but a number of
straggling and often divergent roots which affect the shape and character
of the eventual policy. A.J.P. Taylor has put the problem forcefully.[3]
Explaining that, when young, he had been impressed by a picture of
'Tribal Gods of the nineteenth century, national symbols for which men
would die', he went on:

> The historian, particularly the historian of foreign policy, finds it hard
> to escape the Tribal Gods. We may remind ourselves over and over
> again that the foreign policy of a country is made by a few experts and
> a few rather less expert politicians. We may try to bring out the cross-
> currents which push foreign policy first in one direction, then in
> another. We may resist the assumption that governments are always in
> line with public opinion, and still more the assumption that public
> opinion, even if it can be ascertained, is ever in fact the opinion held by
> everyone in the country. But the Tribal Gods are always breaking in.
> We have to treat foreign policy as a block, a solid lump, if we are going
> to get through the story at all. We write 'the British' when we mean
> 'the few members of the Foreign Office who happened to concern
> themselves with this question'. Great Britain is made to move with the
> ponderous certainty of John Bull. In the end we build up a picture of
> an apostolic succession, in which statesmen moving from one muddle
> to the next display 'the continuity of British foreign policy'. 'The
> British tradition'; 'the British way of life'; 'policy transcending party
> differences' — the incense of these phrases delights the nostrils of the
> Tribal Gods . . . [But] the one continuous thing in British policy is not
> that it has been universally accepted but that there has always been
> disagreement, controversy about it.

Such a statement would be true of all states' foreign policies, even of those
which are ostensibly monolithic in character and do not permit the existence of organised opposition. It is true that the Tribal Gods are strong,
not only because of coercion and propaganda by governments, but also
because of those cloudy images of the state which exist in Bosanquetian

forms amongst the population. The principal domestic complications for governments in making foreign policy derive from two sources: divergent interests within the community, and divergent attitudes amongst officials and ministers. The two are often closely connected, but are usually studied separately.

The divergent domestic interests can often be isolated and clearly seen, though not always at the time of operation. For example, it would have been commercially most unprofitable for the British-based oil companies to cease supplying oil which might go to Rhodesia after the unilateral declaration of independence in 1965. Those companies operated also in South Africa, which they did not wish to antagonise, and from which oil could easily be supplied to Rhodesia. In consequence, the British government was hoodwinked for more than a decade, and part of its foreign policy set at naught, by companies which were overall massive contributors to the British balance of payments, and which, in consequence, were not likely to be closely investigated by British governments of any political complexion. Again, the eruption of Greek-American protest following the Turkish invasion of Cyprus in 1974 was sufficient to cause the US Congress to adopt a pro-Greek and anti-Turkish line, in spite of the conviction of the US administration that Turkey was a vital link in NATO's defence chain. One could illustrate the point also by the constant dilemma of US administrations in recent years, in trying to balance the American need to cultivate Arab oil-producing states against the conviction of the American Jewish community that US commitment to Israel should take precedence. In all these cases, as in so many more, a conflict of interest within the domestic political system was sufficient to cause a major change in the external official behaviour of the state.

Such conflicts will normally reflect themselves amongst the officials who advise governments, sometimes within particular ministries or departments, and sometimes between one ministry and another. Officials will also have their own conflicts, indigenous to the bureaucracy. The United States, with its vast and normally anarchic governmental machine, is particularly rich in this kind of internal disturbance. Other countries with stricter traditions do not provide quite the same brilliant array of examples, though they are to be found in memoirs, and gathered through word of mouth.[4] An economic department may, for example, demand that the asperity of an approach initiated by a foreign office should be toned down, since the state against which the asperity is directed is one with which it is necessary to trade. Behind the economic department, whether brought into consultation or not, will be ranked the trading interests involved; if necessary, they may be called upon to exert their own influence in support of the department. Again, a department wishing to encourage formal relations with another state may suggest a cultural agreement, but this may be opposed by a scientific or educational department because of the complications which such an agreement would create for it. One department may wish to have defence equipment acquired abroad, and another to have it manufactured at home. One may stress employment, another the balance of payments, another the security situation, another the need for the reduction of trade barriers, another the desirability of scientific cooperation, another the effects of investment — all within the same context of relations with a particular state, and all with potential influence upon what will eventually emerge as external behaviour. It does not require much imagination to see that similar disputes can arise in respect of the foreign policy of an apparently monolithic state such as China or the Soviet Union.

The highly pluralist character of official consideration of foreign policy is one of the reasons for so much study in recent years of the decision-making process.[5] The literature invites us to ask whether 'decisions' can ever be isolated, or whether the so-called 'decision-making system' simply lurches from what Taylor would call one muddle to another. Obviously, there will be great differences between states. The spectrum of difference can be seen as having the United States at one end, and some small country with an extremely simple governmental structure (say, Tonga or the Maldive Islands) at the other. The more complex the governmental structure, the more interests one can expect to need satisfying, both within the departments and within the community at large. There will thus be great diversity in practice, because a policy thought out in one section of the government is likely to be challenged in others, and will be subject to objections from those interests which might be adversely affected. Whatever decision emerges from such a process is likely to be at best an approximation to the policy originally suggested.

However, we should not consider that there is something unique about this pluralistic process as applied to foreign policy. It is the normal process through which all governmental policies go before they emerge in public and are put into effect. Some policies, domestic and foreign, may be announced on such public occasions as elections and implemented immediately afterwards; but these are rare, and their implementation will often display the marks of modification through the influence of interests and officials. Broadly speaking, all intended policies are liable to turn into compromises as their implications become clearer.

This does not mean that policy-making, so-called, is simply one muddle after another. The muddles are interspersed by policies which are the result of deliberate thought and careful consultation, and are eventually adopted in a recognisable form. The United States did return the Panama Canal Zone to Panama; Australia did abandon its White Australia policy; Egypt under President Sadat did come to terms with Israel; Portugal did give up its colonies; and the United States and the Soviet Union did arrive at some agreement on strategic arms limitation. These are all examples of substantial changes which were resisted by elements in the community and the governmental machine, but which none the less went into effect.

At the same time, we should recognise that much foreign policy, like much domestic policy, is not the outcome of decisions at all, but is the current expression of official attitudes that have become traditional. These are often of great influence and remarkable persistence. One could cite the official Canadian military opinion in the 1920s that the United States was the potential enemy against which Canada had to arm itself; and the shibboleths about sterling which for so long governed British external financial policy after World War II.[6] These are essentially attitudes built up in one situation, and continuing until new conditions cannot be gainsaid. New attitudes then take their place. In terms of British external economic policy, one can parallel the change to acceptance of a 'floating pound' with equanimity, after decades in which such a concept was anathema, with the conversion of official opinion in and about 1960 to Britain's joining the EEC.[7]

Such instances not only indicate how influential official opinion can be, and how it can change without the fact's being widely known in public; they also show that consistency in the application of outmoded policies may be a cardinal feature of any state's external behaviour.

III

Given that there are both external and internal restraints upon foreign policy, and that these are amongst the roots from which foreign policy grows, let us suppose that we have the task of making foreign policy for state X. The state is not necessarily a major power, but has a fairly wide range of foreign contacts. It is not in any sense isolated from the main currents of international politics. It trades widely, has connections with the superpowers and the major European powers and Japan, is situated near neighbours with whom its relations are close and has some decades of diplomatic experience. It is neither one of the poorest states nor one of the richest. In other words, it is probably typical of the majority of states, though not of all.

To begin with, policy-makers will have to make some estimate of where the state's interests lie. An estimate of interests will not decide how every UN vote should be cast, or what sort of attitude to take in the event of a clash between the superpowers; but it will indicate the directions in which the state's efforts should be exerted, and will give some ranking to the kinds of issues with which the state may be confronted in international forums and associations. It is, however, a difficult task.

First, policy-makers will find that there is no permanent 'national interest' to which they can attach themselves, except for such truisms as that the state's interest lies in peace (i.e., the kind of peace of which its rulers approve), prosperity (i.e., the economic conditions from which its own people gain most) and self-preservation (i.e., the retention of its boundaries and of what its rulers regard as its distinctive institutions). True, its geographical position will require it to pay particular attention to its neighbourhood horizon; but this will not decide what to do in a particular neighbourhood dispute. The quest for national interests in a given period will depend on the characteristics of that period as they affect the state. For example, if there has been a change in the state's trading pattern, this will affect its area of interest: some states will be less important than they used to be, other will be more so. Again, if the state is heavily concerned about national defence, the power which will provide arms on the most advantageous terms (both financial and contractual) will bulk large in its conception of interests.

Second, whatever the policy-makers work out is not likely to be echoed in full by the political forces within the state. Those whose interests lie in exports may be at odds with those to whom imports are of major importance. There may be ideological differences in respect of possible associates and adversaries. There may be considerable volatility in domestic opinion on foreign issues, so that a state which may seem to the planners to be worthwhile as a long-term associate may be publicly criticised in terms of its immediate behaviour. Much will depend on the institutional opportunities for lobbying and obfuscation on the part of dissident interests. In this respect, the processes of the US Congress provide more opportunities than the comparable institutions of almost any other country; but state X may have its own refinements (e.g., there may be the intricate relationships of a royal or near-royal court, as in Morocco, Haiti, Indonesia and the Ivory Coast), and the policy-maker will need to adjust to these if he is to present a set of interests which correspond to local political realities.

Given that some rough indication of interests and where they lie is decided on, there is the practical question of which horizons matter most to the state, i.e., where its efforts should be concentrated. As indicated, neighbours are indispensable, and so are the superpowers — unless that state is so heavily committed to one of them that it can afford to ignore the other. There will also, however, be problems in deciding whether there is a horizon of kindred states, and, if so, which are to be found there, and which are the most suitable to cultivate. Grouping and caucusing in the UN and its specialised agencies induce every state to look for the group which will be most advantageous to it. Quite new states (such as the Pacific island states in recent years) may have regional connections, and may be able to fit in to more than one UN group; but they then have to decide whether membership of more than one will affect opportunities for influence in whichever group seems to count for most. For European and Latin American states, the question of a kindred horizon is more or less settled.

Before state X goes very far, its policy-makers will be faced with the problem of power. This is, in many ways, the central problem of foreign policy, made no easier by the fact that it involves ambiguities and imponderables which require to be dealt with if behaviour is to be effective. Briefly, the policy-makers must ask themselves what sort of power or strength they can bring to international negotiation. However, 'power' is not something that can be measured, even though it may, in certain circumstances, need to be assessed in terms of arms production or capacity to lend. When the policy-makers are thinking of power, it will be essentially in terms of the impact or the 'clout' (as it is widely called) that the power will create. Strength in the abstract is not enough; it is power which will have influence with particular states at particular times that is needed. In the abstract, it is easy to say that the Soviet Union has more power than Tonga, because it is bigger and stronger and more productive; but this does not mean that the Soviet Union can exert its will over Tonga in all situations in which it may wish to do so. Rather, it means that the Soviet Union must find that portion of its power which will be effective in persuading or coercing Tonga into acquiescence, without causing international uproar or damaging the Soviet Union's relations with states that matter to it for other reasons than those which apply in the case of Tonga.

Providing there is some approximation of power (in the sense of resources) to the situation in which it is to apply, even those states which are apparently least powerful may prove to have resources which are relevant. Singapore, for example, is one of the world's smallest states, and its armed strength is negligible. However, it is of much importance in

Asian business and trade, and its leader, Lee Kuan Yew, is noted for his articulacy and shrewdness. The former of these two resources has made Singapore a significant element in international business, as that applies to Southeast Asia, and also in such fields as international civil aviation. The latter gave Lee the role of spokesman for the Afro-Asian caucus at the critical meeting of Commonwealth heads of government in September 1966, when firm conditions were laid down about rebellious Rhodesia. In material terms, Singapore was one of the least powerful Afro-Asian states represented, but Lee was one of the most influential leaders. The two examples show that strength can reside in much more than size or armed force.

Problems of assessing one's own state's power in particular circumstances must always be in the minds of policy-makers. The problem is not one to be ventilated in rhetorical gestures from the presidential balcony or on the hustings, but it is of the essence of foreign policy. Whatever may be said on emotional occasions, the vital issue is what is to be done; and that will depend on the kind of power that can be brought to bear without making the cure worse than the disease. Examples are legion from the experience of the United States, but two are obviously of great moment. One is the fact that the USA had the power to settle the Vietnam war by using nuclear weapons, but refrained from doing so because of possible consequences for Chinese and Russian behaviour. The other is that overwhelming force could have been used against Iran in the early months of 1980, when hostages were being held in the US embassy; but this might have led to the death of the hostages, and would have been counterproductive for future relations between the USA and Iran, a key country on the borders of the Soviet Union. In both these situations the US government, finding that military force was not the resource which would obtain what it wanted, turned to diplomacy as the means of salvaging its position.

It is at the level of diplomacy that interests and 'clout' come together. At any given time, state X will be involved in a variety of diplomatic exercises, corresponding roughly to the horizons which appear before it. It may have contracted alliances which serve to defend it in regional terms, but which require that obligations to other members be met. It may have trade treaties which, in certain circumstances (such as those which involve the states of Eastern Europe in relation to the Soviet Union), constitute its main preoccupation. The groups and caucuses of the UN and the specialised agencies may be the principal means through which the state can exert influence, if it is poor, lacks a widespread diplomatic network and considers that its 'clout' can come only from effective coalition with others.

As we saw in Essay 3, there is a wide range of diplomatic occasions on which influence can be exerted. They range from 'summits' of various kinds to day-to-day converse between officials and the envoys accredited to their state. Amongst the decisions made by state X's policy-makers will be those about which venue to use for a particular initiative, and what sort of behaviour to regard as appropriate in the circumstances. The United States, for example, will not act in the same way in the closed confines of the OECD as it does in the propaganda-saturated public atmosphere of the UN Security Council. While state X will not have as many resources to deploy as the United States, it will still have choices about what to do, and where and how to do it.

Above all, the policy-makers and leaders of state X will have to make decisions, from time to time, about the extent of rhetoric in their policy, in comparison with the extent of calculation and careful effort. It is possible, of course, that calculation may indicate a need for rhetoric, since there seems to be nothing else to do in a particular situation; but the policy-makers must try to avoid the attitude which, according to Roger Fisher, afflicts the United States in too many circumstances:

> Foreign policy making is seen as producing an attitude that is not merely appropriate for a particular situation; the objective is to produce an all-purpose attitude which will serve for many different situations over a long period of time. Consistency is deemed a great virtue of foreign policy. A statement of our position is deemed better the more often it has been said before. By the time an attitude has been stated and restated by four Presidents — by the time it has become a platitude — it has become a firmly entrenched bit of United States foreign policy. And by that time it may be worse than useless. Whatever merit there may have been in the posture when first adopted, little good is accomplished by repeating slogans such as 'no appeasement', 'open covenants openly arrived at', 'we must honour our commitments', and 'we are in favour of the United Nations'. Such maxims take on a life of their own and become substitutes for thought. The conduct of foreign affairs is seen less as the exercise of a governmental skill and more as the articulation of an all-purpose answer.[8]

Just as calculation may indicate the need for rhetoric, so it may indicate that, in a vast, heterogeneous state such as the USA, only slogans can be enunciated in public, so as to avoid undue controversy which will harm negotiation. Perhaps state X will find that only opposition to neo-colonialism and racism, or assertion of the virtues of a particular religion, will be acceptable to the public. But the policy-makers will find that this is insufficient for the conduct of a foreign policy. They will have to work out methods of external behaviour that complement it, in the sense that they provide allied and associated states with the reactions which they require if they are to continue to be associates. The balance between rhetoric and substantial activity has to be struck afresh at each stage of state X's progress.

IV

Foreign policy is not only hard to do — as state X's needs show — but also hard to study. If we are to recognise and analyse significant change in the foreign policy of the states with which we are concerned, we need to deal with certain problems.

One of these is the problem of which forces we take into account when we are assessing the external behaviour of a particular state. The problem becomes more acute, the more complex the sociopolitical organisation of the state. As already indicated, it is hardly ever sufficient to consider only the activity of foreign offices. That activity has to be seen in relation to the whole official apparatus of a state, and the activities of other government departments and bureaux that affect external behaviour; it has also to be seen in relation to the major political interests within the community, so that foreign policy becomes a kind of resultant of major social forces (or interests) concerned with relations with other states. A crucial question arises in connection with states that have a capitalist economic system. Marxists maintain that these states, by their very nature, cannot have a foreign policy which is fully under the control of governments, even when affected by pressure from within the domestic political system; instead, the major decisions will be made in the interests of monopoly capitalists, whose needs will, in the last analysis, govern the behaviour which governments exhibit. In this sense, from a Marxist standpoint, there is little difference between domestic and external policy, since the interests of capitalist forces will always prevail.

In respect of major 'developed' countries, the distinction between foreign and domestic policy is of little account, since local capitalists are those whose interests are presumed to decide both, except in cases in which the Marxist analysts maintain that local capitalists are merely 'fronts' for capitalists in the United States. In respect of 'under-developed' countries, however, the latter kind of assertion becomes more important. Since there is, by definition, little local mobilisation of capital, local capitalists are held to be merely 'compradores', i.e., those acting on behalf of greater counterparts in the developed countries; consequently, it is assumed that whatever policies the state produces cannot even be indigenous, but must proceed from external sources. Those states which do not have socialist systems (and those which, while they have socialist systems, do not approve of the policies of the Soviet Union or China or Albania, whichever is the state favoured most by the Marxists putting forward the argument) are taken to be puppets of monopoly capitalists of the imperialist kind which Lenin identified.

For anyone seeking the roots of foregin policy, this is a formidable indictment. In abstract terms, given its assumptions, it is difficult to refute. If there are certain kinds of states which are fated by their history to act in accordance with the interests of monopoly capitalists in their own or in other countries, then one need look no further for the origins of their foreign policies. They cannot act in any different way, except perhaps in unimportant details of style and method, in rhetoric and obfuscation. Should we look further? It would save time and effort if we did not.

In fact, however, both time and effort are needed, in order to see whether the behaviour of states actually corresponds to what is postulated. In respect of major developed countries, external behaviour in trade and related matters is clearly affected by the interests of big firms; but it is also affected by the interests of farmers, trade unionists and local groups, not to speak of conservationists and a variety of others. French and Japanese trade policies, for example, are very much affected in this way. Big firms normally have influence but rarely dominance. So far as the assertion of domination by American monopoly capitalists is concerned, there is sufficient evidence of divergence between US policy on the one hand and that of states such as West Germany, France and Japan on the other — especially in regard to economic links with communist states — to make the assertion suspect.

Of course, a Marxist could regain his position by saying that the era of monopoly capitalism involves clashes between the capitalist forces of one state and those of others, which will be reflected in foreign policy; and/or that the capitalists of the USA, Japan, France, etc., in spite of these clashes, prefer unison in overall protective bodies such as NATO and OECD to having their states picked off, one after another, by the just assaults of the forces of progress. Such replies are normally, to a large extent, reassertions of the original proposition. They do not deal in any detail with the policy-making processes or the external behaviour of the states in question.

The proposition is more formidable, and more widely accepted, in regard to states of the Third World. To a certain degree, history is on its side. In the days of the United Fruit Company's operations amongst the 'banana republics' of Central America, and those of the Firestone Rubber Company in Liberia, the states acted very much as the dominant companies wished. They were small, insignificant states, with little or no support which they could muster if they disagreed with the companies which in the 1920s and 30s monopolised their slender economic resources. The situation of underdeveloped countries today presents a great contrast.

The nationalisation of copper mines in Zambia and of the oil wells in various OPEC countries, the permanent repatriation of phosphate profits to Nauru, and a variety of other such actions following the virtual expropriation of British assets in Argentina, indicate that there is now far more power in the hands of minor states than ever before. Indeed, the closest parallel in the contemporary world is with the actions of similar states in successfully refusing to accept continued undue influence by the Soviet Union over their defence and economic policies. Indonesia and Egypt are states which, in pursuit of what they conceived to be their own interests, turned against the Soviet Union without incurring significant damage.

It seems reasonable to assert that, in all these instances, it is the existence of the sovereign state that matters most, and that the influence of either monopoly capitalists or Soviet provision of arms is not, in itself, sufficient to decide policy. No doubt there are other instances in which it does prove sufficient. But the contrary instances are so striking and so numerous that the proposition ceases to have the self-evident appearance with which it began.

For underdeveloped countries, there is now some safety in numbers. With such an array at the UN and elsewhere, it has become more difficult for either monopoly capitalists or the diplomats of superpowers to exert the Firestone type of influence. Undoubtedly, influence is still present, since one must expect that any major interest within a state's economy will be influential; but there is a difference between exerting influence as a local lobby, along with other lobbyists, and deciding ultimate policy as a matter of course. Whether one regards multinational corporations as demonic influences or as relatively useful agencies of economic growth — and the performance of such firms as Unilever in West Africa and Booker Bros. in Guyana would support the latter view — it is the case that they now have to deal with fully sovereign states in a Third-World context, and no longer with the Liberias and Guatemalas of the earlier period, or with acquiescent colonial governments. Similarly, a superpower has to take note of the opinion of Third-World states at large when attempting coercive action against any one of them.[9]

In such a situation one can see the sovereign state exercising the functions described in Essay 2. States today, even at the lowest level of national income, present certain obstacles to any attempt at external coercion. This does not mean that external coercion is impossible; clearly, it is still possible to subvert or bribe a government, arrange a *coup d'état*, threaten to 'teach a lesson' by military force (as the Chinese did to Vietnam), or otherwise exert the strongest pressure. But it is reasonable to suggest that, across the range of sovereign states, such violent and near-violent forms of influence are becoming less effective than in earlier times. States which deliver a variety of modern services and provide significant protection in the economic and military fields — as most Third-World states do, even though provision for the people on lowest incomes and with fewest prospects is usually poor — are difficult to deal with by means of coercion. They normally have administrations which, while retaining links with traditional culture, are modern-minded in many respects, and can act as articulate and influential members of Third-World groups. The state's functions of provision and representation play an important part in enabling it to mobilise domestic support to preserve its autonomy, in contrast with the Moroccos and Persias of the past. The change is in no sense absolute; but it is a change none the less, and gives the sovereign state more chance of survival than it had before.

The problems of study created by foreign policy include not only the dogmatic proposition that states are not really in charge of their foreign policies because this is the era of monopoly capitalism, but also the milder, less forceful suggestion that it is 'state-centric' to think in terms of foreign policy, when the interdependence of states is constantly increasing, and their prospects of independent state action are thereby reduced. In particular, such a view challenges the notion that external *official* behaviour is all we need to study. Other forms of external behaviour, e.g., by locally domiciled firms, may be just as significant as any official act, it is argued; and there are cases in which this is true.

A third problem of study is especially important when one is looking for the roots of foreign policy. It concerns the connections between foreign and domestic policy. As readers of the preceding essays and this one will know, I make little distinction between these in terms of either their origins (except, of course, that foreigners bulk large in foreign policy questions) or their procedures (except that diplomacy, as an activity, is distinctive, though it is obviously related to aspects of domestic political management — e.g., in cases of conflict such as industrial disputes — where some kind of mediating role is called for). It has never seemed to me worth making a clear distinction. Much of the argument amongst academics over whether both domestic and foreign policy should be studied together, or whether one is part of a discipline called 'political science' and the other of one called 'international relations', is simply a case of academic politics, i.e., of specialists in differing fields who do not wish to acknowledge kinship with, or perhaps inferiority to, others who are entrenched and insist on maintaining their positions. As Essay 1 shows, I think that domestic and foreign policies are both part of politics; that the study of politics is best seen as a unified affair because politics has a basic dynamic in scarcity; and that the framework of analysis involving inequality, interests and authority can be used with profit for both.

There is, however, a certain advantage in discussing the relations between domestic and foreign policy because it helps to establish the significance of the sovereign state within the international system. Briefly, most of the things which states do abroad are the consequences of, or closely connected with, the things which they do at home. The most obvious examples are in the sphere of economic policy. It is impossible to separate the interests which the state professes abroad from interests at home. Whether the issue is one of reduction of tariff and non-tarriff barriers, or the abolition of preferences, or the conditions under which the exchange rate will alter, or those under which foreign investment will be permitted, or the extent to which fishing grounds or coast-wise shipping or the carriage of domestic air passengers or a licence to conduct banking business are to be made available to foreign operators, the issue as presented to other states will be the resultant of domestic politics. The state will be called upon to provide official sanction to those interests which have won the domestic debate. Foreign economic policy can never be divorced from domestic policy; indeed, there are those who maintain that it is unwise for governments even to have separate departments of trade or other aspects of external economic policy, and that a single department should handle the affairs of a particular commodity or service, as they arise both at home and abroad.

Much the same can be said, though perhaps with rather less emphasis, about defence policy. The kind of military face which a state exhibits to other states is obviously a highly important aspect of its external behaviour. Its nature will be governed not simply by military leaders' perception of a 'threat' and of the resources needed to meet it, but by a variety of domestic considerations. In many countries, the issue of conscription or 'the draft' is a matter of great domestic concern. Whether the budgetary allocation for defence should be increased or reduced is a highly contentious issue in domestic terms, since an increase may mean less money for domestic programmes, while a reduction may lead either to an increase in those domestic programmes or a decrease in taxes. How the money allotted to defence is to be spent is itself not one domestic issue, but a series of such issues. There will be argument about where to spend it (since military installations, airfields, bases, academies, etc., boost the economies of the areas in which they are located); what to buy with it (especially as between naval, air and ground equipment, and between weapons, vehicles and communications systems, to go no further); how it is to be divided between equipment and manpower; and how much of the equipment should be bought abroad, and how much at home. A budget decision about the defence vote is, in effect, a whole set of decisions about domestic and foreign policy. The fact is not lost on legislators or on those domestic interests which are concerned.

There may also be domestic interests which affect foreign policy in a less material way than those concerned with economic and defence policy. They comprise those people who, on ethnic or ideological or religious grounds, find particular foreign states highly attractive or essentially damnable. All immigrant countries (which make up a large proportion of the states of the world; as we have seen, the Frances and Japans are rare) have experience of this kind of domestic effect. The US Congress, for example, was passing resolutions about Irish and Polish and Hungarian independence, in response to pressures from local groups, long before World War I; Northern Ireland still creates an Irish dimension in American politics. Countries like Canada and Australia, which received many anti-communist immigrants from Europe after World War II, are aware of the domestic significance of pressures from Ukrainians and Croats and others whose *bête noire* is the Soviet Union. These are cases in which policies of aversion are urged on a state from within. Conversely, the pressures of American and Canadian Jews about Israel, and of Australian and other Catholics about South Vietnam and Biafra, are reminders that domestic interests may be rallied to call for support of this or that foreign state.

Such an assembly of domestic effects on foreign policy suggests that domestic and foreign are simply two sides of the same coin — that, when a state behaves in a certain manner towards other states, it is expressing domestic forces which seek advantage from whatever influence can be brought to bear abroad. Such a conclusion would be a long way from

A.J.P. Taylor's characterisation of foreign policy as being made by 'a few experts and a few rather less expert politicians'. The experts are still there, and the politicians have, if anything, increased in number and interests. What has changed most, however, since the brave days of Lord Palmerston, is the extent of public concern about foreign policy, expressed in the number and variety of interests which may gain or lose from particular policies. This increase corresponds to the increase in the state's provision of services to its citizens, in response to domestic pressures and a heightened awareness of what is done by other states. Inevitably, the increased domestic activities of the state necessitate increased activity abroad, both to protect and enhance domestic interests which may otherwise be aggrieved. Whether it is to obtain markets for an automobile industry or an airline which has been established or expanded through state action, or to refuse to recognise the incorporation of the Baltic states in the Soviet Union or of East Timor in Indonesia, a state's external behaviour will reflect whatever has become consensus, or majority opinion, or simply dominant political interests, in the domestic field. There will be other considerations too, as we have seen. Basically, however, the roots of foreign policy rest in the people of the state, as those express themselves politically.

V

At least one final problem remains to be discussed in relation to foreign policy. It is that of morality.[10] What is good behaviour between states? How can one say that a particular action would be wrong? Can we even speak of morality when we are dealing with states, not with individual human beings? There is no doubt that people constantly discuss the morality of particular instances of external official behaviour, and express their approval or disapproval. Is this a waste of time?

Machiavelli thought that it was, in the sense that, while we could work out what was right in the abstract, we were likely to cause ourselves trouble in personal life if we stuck to it; a ruler would get his state into even worse trouble:

> . . . how we live is so far removed from how we ought to live, that he who abandons what is done for what ought to be done, will rather learn to bring about his own ruin than his preservation. A man who wishes to make a profession of goodness in everything must necessarily come to grief among so many who are not good. Therefore it is

necessary for a prince, who wishes to maintain himself, to learn how not to be good, and to use it and not use it according to the necessities of the case.[11]

The essence of the problem lies in Machiavelli's use of the clause, 'who wishes to maintain himself', to describe his prince. The same description can be used about the rulers of any state, and of the people within the state. In each case they wish, not only to preserve the state in being, but also to preserve themselves in that state of life, with those boundaries, privileges, opportunities and advantages, which they enjoy at the time. If mankind were the body of persons whose standard of life had to be preserved, state behaviour would be different; but it is the standard of life within the state itself that must be preserved, even though this means that others will be discriminated against. The state is, in effect, a machine for protection and preservation of what its citizens regard as rightly theirs. It is also, of course, a machine for enabling the rulers to rule; their task would, however, be far harder if they did not take account of the most pressing demands made upon them. The morality of a state is that of success and preservation. Whatever succeeds in preserving and maintaining the state and its provisions will be good morality. Each state takes this attitude in greater or less degree, and with more or less stridency in utterance.

There would be no difficulty in putting together, in the abstract, other moralities which the state might adopt. As we have seen, there could be one embracing the whole of mankind, and demanding that all human beings be treated alike. There could be one which laid down rules for state behaviour, and applied sanctions when those rules were transgressed. (This is what the UN Charter does; but precept and practice differ.) There could be one which recognised the absolute primacy of the state, and encouraged, instead of deprecating, conflict between one state and another: 'each for himself, and the devil take the hindmost'. There could be one which said that, morally speaking, states were of no account, and that individuals had the full right to defy their states when they considered that morality was being breached. All of these have had their advocates; but those advocates' voices have traditionally been of little avail when the application of their precepts would seem to damage the interests of significant groups of people within the state, or lead to its destruction.

In practice, there is a kind of low-level morality which states recognise in most of their dealings with one another. The development of this kind of morality would seem to offer the best hope for further application of moral principles in the future. It is a morality based on common interest. If something can be seen to be clearly in the interests of all states, or a group of them — such as the rules for navigation at sea, or the arrangements of the Universal Postal Union — then all will be prepared to accept it, and to regard as wrong any action which goes against it. Exceptions arise in time of war and on occasions when states lack the technical means to carry out their duties; but, by and large, the morality which arises from mutual expediency is adhered to. It is doubtful if anything more than this can be expected from states. Only if they extend their sense of common interest beyond transport and communications (as they have done, for example, in some areas of trade and of the use of the sea in recent years) are we likely to see a more consistent and widespread morality prevail.

In the meantime, the individual citizen will continue to ask whether his own and other states' foreign policies are moral, and will draw his own conclusions. He cannot be blamed for this. At every stage of his life he is called upon to approve or disapprove of a whole range of public activities. In some countries he is ordered into the streets, or otherwise attracted to great assemblies, in order to demonstrate his approval or disapproval as part of his loyalty to the state. The question of whether he approves of foreign policy is really another aspect of what he thinks of governmental activity. Perhaps he can be consoled with two observations when he asks why relations between states cannot be conducted according to the standards which he thinks should be applied to private life. One is that group morality, in the sense of insistence on the superiority of the self-serving claims of a particular group (similar to the claims made for itself by each sovereign state), is frequent within the domestic affairs of his own society, and is not confined to international politics. The second is that, according to Aristotle, 'the ruled may be compared to flute-makers: rulers are like flute-players who use what the flute-makers make'.[12] In other words, the roots of foreign policy lie in great part amongst the people, expressing their needs and wishes in terms of what the state can do. If the state is to do better, according to their personal morality, it is for them to say.

Notes

1. John Locke, *The Second Treatise of Civil Government*, ed. J.W. Gough (Oxford, 1964), p. 73. Although Locke's kind words about leaving the exercise of the federative power to those who have it committed to them might be thought to suggest a group of people, separate from the executive, who manage this power on their own, this was not what he intended. He thought that 'to have the force of the public . . . under different

commands . . . would be apt some time or other to cause disorder and ruin' (p. 74). So we do not need a separate government for foreign policy. At the same time, we can recognise in Locke's statement an echo of the view that foreign policy is too important to be left to politicians.

2. Four books which give the reader contrasting views of what constitutes an international system, and how to assess it when it has been discovered, are Morton Kaplan, *System and Process in International Politics* (New York, 1957); F.H. Hinsley, *Power and the Pursuit of Peace* (Cambridge, 1967); Martin Wight, *Systems of States*, ed. Hedley Bull (Leicester, 1977); and Richard N. Rosecrance, *Action and Reaction in World Politics* (Boston, 1963).

3. A.J.P. Taylor, *The Troble Makers: Dissent over Foreign Policy 1792-1939* (London, 1958), pp. 11-12.

4. A British example, involving conflict over how to handle relations with India and other Commonwealth countries in 1948, will be found in Joe Garner, *The Commonwealth Office 1925-68* (London, 1978), pp. 300-2. Like most such disputes, this was unknown to the general public.

5. A good account of this is B.P. White, 'Decision-making analysis' in Trevor Taylor (ed.), *Approaches and Theory in International Relations* (London, 1978). My feeling is that awareness of the complexities of decision-making is not so recent as White suggests; however, the intensity with which it is studied certainly is.

6. For the first of these, see James Eayrs, *In Defence of Canada: From the Great War to the Great Depression* (Toronto, 1964), ch. III; and for the second, Susan Strange, *Sterling and British Policy* (London, 1970).

7. See Miriam Camps, *Britain and the European Community 1955-1963* (London, 1964).

8. Roger Fisher, *International Conflict for Beginners* (New York, 1970), p. 4.

9. The point was illustrated when the Soviet Union sent troops into Afghanistan in 1979-80. However, some forms of intervention by major powers are not universally condemned in the Third World, notably those by France in Africa. This is presumably because the majority of francophone African states approve of what the French are doing to their more unruly neighbours, and make it clear to other Third-World countries that they do not wish complaints to be made. This is a case of how one horizon can blot out another. France is still of major importance to its ex-colonies, whereas, on the whole, Belgium, Britain and Portugal are not.

10. What follows is largely a condensation of my paper, 'Morality, Interests and Rationalisation', in Ralph Pettman (ed.), *Moral Claims in World Affairs* (London, 1979), pp. 36-51.

11. Machiavelli, *The Prince*, ch. XV; and there is also the notorious ch. XVIII.

12. *The Politics of Aristotle*, trs. Ernest Barker (Oxford, 1948), p. 106.

5   INTEGRATION AND ITS MYTHS

This essay is about an episode in the study of international politics — not an entirely self-contained episode, but one which clearly had its day and may not occupy the attention of specialists for much longer. It was concerned with questions of political integration, or regional integration, or political community, depending on which writer one takes as the standard. Essentially, it involved study of the conditions under which political units would combine with one another to form larger units; in this sense, it was part of a long line of enquiries concerned with such topics as federalism. This line is likely to continue since there will never be any lack of speculation about whether this and that community might unite, and under what conditions. The episode to which I refer was, however, largely confined to the 1960s and 70s, and will probably not recur with the same intensity, or with the same concentration upon a particular set of circumstances. It is important because it tells us something about the sovereign state, and something about the way in which people pursue the study of international politics, especially in the United States.

I

The integrationist period, or episode, was one in which American theorists, interested for a variety of reasons in the closer association of the states of Western Europe, tried very hard both to foster that association and also to learn from the experience of the European Community what might be the conditions of successful integration between states at large. Having embarked upon this investigation, they turned their attention to other parts of the world in which integration might take place (such as Central America and East Africa), and attempted to apply the categories, concepts and causation which they had learnt from postwar Western Europe and from what they considered to be comparable historical examples.

In its preoccupation with Western Europe, this movement amongst scholars had more than scholarly curiosity to support it. From the end of

World War II, there had been an official American interest in closer connection between the countries of Western Europe. It was American policy, first to use such resources as food, fuel and transport to best advantage so as to provide relief throughout the prostrate Western Europe of the immediate postwar period; and then, from 1947 through the Marshall Plan, to foster rapid recovery under conditions which rationalised the available capital resources and enabled not one, but all, of the countries which had been involved in the war to rehabilitate themselves. The OEEC (Organization for European Economic Cooperation) was the organ through which the Marshall Plan was administered:

> Over and over, the Americans prodded the Europeans to give the OEEC more power, more authority and a single, vigorous executive head. When visiting Congressmen asked the Marshall Planners what they were trying to do, they would answer, 'We're trying to pull them together, we're trying to integrate them.' 'Integration' was a convenient word and each successive delegation asked sternly, 'How far have you got with integration now?' as if expecting the Marshall Plan to pull out of its desk drawer a draft constitution for Europe and a design for a European flag.[1]

Much of this concern arose from the wish that Western Europe should not follow Eastern Europe and become a dependency of the Soviet Union. To a large extent, US anxiety was stilled by the formation of NATO in 1949, with its commitment of both American and European forces against any move westwards by the Soviet Union. However, the desire for European integration remained. It was founded on both general and particular propositions. The general proposition was that Europe had been the source of previous wars, and that, unless the European states learned to live together in peace, they would cause further trouble for the world at large. This included the view that, while the whole of Europe could not be involved in any move towards integration, because of Soviet control of the eastern half of the continent, this very fact made the need for integration of the western half even more urgent. The particular proposition was that West Germany must be indissolubly bound to its western neighbours so as to preclude any deal with the Soviet Union.

There were thus strong politico-military reasons why Americans should seek, and be officially encouraged to seek, to become more knowledgeable about how the integrative process could proceed in Western Europe. There were also economic reasons. Throughout the

1930s it had been painfully apparent that the depression was being prolonged by the autarchic nationalism practised by one European country against another; one of the objectives of Cordell Hull's postwar economic policy had been to liberalise trading relations between European states. The postwar relief programmes and the Marshall Plan had shown that Western Europe could operate effectively as a group of countries sharing common resources and workir g in unison. It was hoped that 'Europe' would become quickly effective as an economic unit.

Along with these political, military and economic reasons for interest in integration went another which might be called intellectual. It had been widely apparent during World War II in Britain and the United States. This was the conviction that, especially but not solely in Europe, undisciplined nationalism was a force to be dreaded, and that the future of world peace, and the general development of mankind, demanded some restriction upon what was still called, in most contexts, the 'nation state'.[2]

It is fair to say that when a scholarly interest in integration became active, it had behind it a good deal of criticism of the sovereign state as an institution — to an extent that one of the most creative members of the movement, Amitai Etzioni, could put the matter in such uncompromising terms as these:

> We have all grown up in the period in which nationalism reached its peak. It still seems a potent historical factor, with new nations established by the month — seventeen in 1960 alone . . . We are likely not to notice that the heyday of nationalism is over; that most peoples desiring national status have already achieved it; and that many nations even now are engaged in the very processes that will overcome the severe handicaps nationalism imposes on their economic, military, political and even cultural well-being.
>
> The trend of the future is toward establishment of supranational communities, whose nation members, like the members of smaller communities, are in general agreement on how their community ought to be run and what goals it ought to pursue and who share an effective supranational government. Most important of all: members of such communities give up the use of violence as a means of settling conflicts among themselves and establish political institutions to safeguard peaceful handling of conflicts that occur.[3]

Such powerful urges towards the study of integration gave Europe a special significance for integration theorists, concentrating their attention on the origins of the European Community (EC) and giving them special reasons for observing closely the way in which the Community developed.[4] The element of policy has never been far from the interests of integration theorists, few of whom, according to their chronicler Charles Pentland, would accept that explanation is the sole or sufficient purpose of theory. 'Indeed, normative positions are rarely, if at all, disguised in their writings. Integration itself is assumed to be a good thing — a proposition which is understandable if not exactly self-evident.'[5]

They were also animated by a particular kind of scholarly urge, that which attempts to attain measurement and precision. 'We were stimulated by two otherwise unrelated trends:', writes Ernst Haas, 'the flowering in the United States of systematic social science and the blooming in Europe of political efforts to build a united continent, to integrate Western Europe at least.'[6] Under such pressures, the scholars had incentives to work out schemes, measurements, indices and the like with which to assess the progress of Western Europe towards integration, and to create an appearance of generality, inevitability and approval in that process as it might occur elsewhere. Although Western Europe remained the centre of interest, attempts were made to take the analysis further so that it became a generalised proposition, subject to modification in terms of local areas, but with a kind of general presumption that the example of Western Europe showed that, in advanced societies, the sovereign state had become a hindrance rather than a help to better living, and that integration — in terms of the 'supranationalism' built into the EC's charter — represented the wave of the future.

I do not mean to suggest that every integrationist took this line. The best (men such as Ernst Haas, Karl Deutsch, Joseph Nye and Donald Puchala) were aware of the limitations of the integrationist formula, and were concerned to show that European conditions could not be fully reproduced elsewhere. However, in many cases the troops outdistanced the generals, in the sense that middle-level practitioners of international relations in the USA found it difficult to avoid sweeping applications of the idea of integration and infected their students accordingly.[7] There is always something intoxicating about a new idea, especially when it can be turned to professional advantage; and this was certainly true for a time of the theory of integration.

Before proceeding to critical examination of the integration movement, it would be advisable to indicate the groups within it. According to Bruce Russett,[8] there are four schools of thought, each of which has its own notion of what constitutes integration. The first, which consists of those early advocates assembled in Atlantic Union and World Federalism, and dates back to World War II, concentrates upon supranational institutions (i.e., those which are superimposed upon existing sovereign states so as to create a new structure which limits their power and replaces it in certain vital respects), gives relatively little attention to where loyalties lie and trusts to federal institutions to bind people together. It is essentially in the line of descent of earlier schemes of federation. The second, widely known as 'neo-functionalist', has developed around Haas, following the earlier work of Mitrany and others. It places its emphasis upon those very questions of loyalty, in attempting to show how the effect of successful functional operations by supranational bodies causes a change of loyalty on the part of interested elites, who, in their attachment to the new supranational institutions, will carry the common people with them in due course. The third, growing out of Deutsch's work, is sometimes called 'transactionalist' because of its emphasis on the growth of transactions between states as a precondition of their movement towards integration. It is concerned with the avoidance of war under conditions of continued voluntary association. The fourth (hardly a group, since it is described as consisting of Russett himself) embodies the notion of 'responsiveness, or the probability that requests emanating from one state to the other will be met favourably'.[9]

II

One of the difficulties in approaching integrationist theory is that of definition. Most of us would have no difficulty in accepting a common-sense definition such as that provided by Donald Puchala: he defines 'regional integration' as 'the merger of two or more states to form a new and larger state'.[10] This is the sort of integration which occurred in Italy and Germany in the nineteenth century, and it is what most of us can readily understand. It provides an effective end-point to the process, and indicates that a new unit has been created within the international political system as it is normally understood. In this essay, it will be assumed that, if there is any genuine progress towards integration in a particular situation, it will emerge in terms of a new and larger state, or will be so clearly moving in that direction as to make the end-point inevitable.

However, that is not how integration has looked to the major theorists of the movement. Karl Deutsch, for example, says that integration 'is a relationship between units in which they are mutually interdependent, and jointly produce system properties which they would separately lack',[11] and follows this with a selection of 'political communities', each of which is said to be 'a collection of political actors whose inter-dependence is sufficient to make a substantial difference to the outcome of some of each other's relevant decisions'.[12] These communities, which include, according to Deutsch, 'communities of conflict', can obviously be made to include almost any kind of continuing relationship between two or more states, and have little to do with the more formal and tangible definition given by Puchala.

The other most notable figure amongst the integrationist theorists, Ernst Haas, is a little nearer to Puchala than Deutsch, but not much. In 1961 he defined political community as a 'terminal condition', which existed 'when there is likelihood of internal peaceful change in a setting of contending groups with mutually antagonistic claims'. The process of attaining this condition among nation-states he called '*integration*, the process whereby political actors in several distinct national settings are persuaded to shift their loyalties, expectations and political activities towards a new and larger centre, whose institutions possess or demand jurisdiction over the pre-existing national states' (my emphasis).[13] Nine years later he made another 'stab at a definition':

> The study of regional integration is concerned with explaining how and why states cease to be wholly sovereign, how and why they voluntarily mingle, merge and mix with their neighbours so as to lose the factual attributes of sovereignty while acquiring new techniques for resolving conflict between themselves. Regional cooperation, organisation, systems, and subsystems may describe steps on the way; but they should not be confused with the resulting condition.[14]

These definitions make the whole operation a good deal more complicated than it would otherwise be. Apart from whether integration, to be regarded as such, must be 'peaceful' and 'voluntary' (see below), there is also the awkward question of whether integration is a condition or a process, or both. On the whole, the theorists maintain that it is a process, although Haas does assign a 'terminal condition' to it, which might be thought to bring it to the same end-point as Puchala's. In his more recent definition, however, Haas speaks of this termination as the situation in which 'states cease to be wholly sovereign'; the presence of the world 'wholly' means that, in any given instance, the loss of *some* sovereignty (such as is often regarded as occurring in the making of any treaty of alliance) presumably shows that the process of integration is in motion.

If integration is to be seen as a process rather than a condition (or as a process devoid of an end-point), then the field is wide open to suggestions that almost anything which we normally call 'connection' or 'cooperation' or 'association' between states is part of the process of integration. To argue like this (as Haas seems to, though one cannot be quite sure) is to rid the word 'integration' of any distinctive meaning. The ordinary experience of states provides ample evidence of these forms of achieving closer relations with one another, yet nobody involved would regard the process as one of integration. It is well known that a move towards closer relations may be followed by one in the other direction, so that states become accustomed to a fairly constant process of steps both forward and back in their connections with each other. There may be increasing contacts between two states, yet this may have no significance in terms of any permanent change in their basic relationship as separate entities.

The problems are not simply semantic, but also concern the substance of what some theorists regard as the very stuff of integration. Deutsch's school is much concerned with 'transactions' which may not in the first instance be those between governments — they begin with mail flows, people's visits to other countries, etc. — but which soon make the contacts between governments, following private transactions, matters of some significance. These provide, it is said, the basis on which integration proceeds. Yet, if integration is viewed in the terms stated by Puchala, transactions between the United States and the two states closest to it geographically — Mexico and Canada — can be seen as substantial in themselves but as providing no basis at all (quite the contrary) for merger in order to form a new and larger state. To put the point bluntly, if one thinks of integration as a process, then almost any increase in contacts, whether private or official, can be pressed into service as evidence that the process has begun between particular states, and that it is well under way as new contacts appear to develop.

Russett's useful four-fold distinction shows that, while each school of theorists is moving in the same direction, some fast and some slowly,[15] with some looking for signs here and some there, the general vagueness of definition means that any critic is caught in something of a 'Catch-22' position. If he insists that integration is to be defined as the merger of states to form new ones, he will be told that he has neglected the whole process by which the merger is achieved, and has, in any case, based his definition upon an outcome which may never occur; his criticism is thus beside the point. If, on the other hand, he accepts the notion of process as the significant one, he will be unable to brand any sort of connection or association as irrelevant to the notion of integration; instead, he will find himself surrounded by ingenious speculations, about whether this or that trivial, humdrum connection really contributes towards the desired end.

In spite of this 'Catch-22' predicament, it seems to me that there is no point in talking about 'integration' unless one is somewhere near the dictionary definitions, and recognises integration as the sort of thing that happened to the minor German states in 1871 and, earlier, did not happen to the Holy Roman Empire. Further, it is important not to regard the creation even of some so-called supranational institutions as necessarily leading to integration as an end-point, in the sense of the creation of a new sovereign state. As we shall see, the existence of these, first in the ECSC and then in the EC, has not led to the subjugation of member-states in matters which they regard as vital, and does not, in itself, lead necessarily to any further steps towards the creation of a political union under some kind of single authority. If there is to be no movement towards a single body, no amount of interconnection, consultation, joint management and the like can be said to attain, or even to be in the process of attaining, integration as it would be understood by the man in the street, and as it might entail some change in his loyalties.

There is a further problem of definition, arising from Haas's emphasis upon integration as 'voluntary' and influenced by 'persuasion'; elsewhere in his 1970 article he speaks of 'the voluntary creation of larger political units each of which self-consciously eschews the use of force in the relations between the participating units and groups'. There is to be a limitation of study to 'noncoercive' efforts at integration. How realistic is this? As Puchala says, 'it is hardly necessary to point out to anyone familiar with the history of international relations that peaceful regional integration is a relatively rare phenomenon'.[16] Yet it appears to be characteristic of integration theorists (especially Haas and Deutsch) that, because they are seeking peace in situations in which undisciplined sovereign states might go to war, and yet are restricted by their preoccupation with the EC from assuming some sort of integration due to conquest, they confine themselves to cases — actual and imaginary — in which states voluntarily come together. If we assume that the study of the process of integration is to be taken seriously and scientifically, there are good reasons for not confining the operation to peaceful and voluntary situations. Three in particular may be described.

The first is simply that so many cases of integration have resulted from coercion. To omit these cases would be to restrict the field unduly, thus inviting speculation in the void — a tendency to which is widespread amongst scholars, and needs frequently to be curbed.

The second is that, if we think of integration as involving the drawing together of previously sovereign states under a superior institution which controls all or part of their activities, the effects will be much the same in certain vital respects, whether the union results from coercion or persuasion. If all the railway systems are to be brought under one control, or the coal mines to be rationalised, or common rates of taxation to be levied, or if the entry to schools and universities is to be the same, or if there is to be a common standard for the medical profession, the impact upon the citizen will be very similar. There will, of course, be some differences: particular interests may be more influential under one set of conditions than under the other, and the atmosphere of political life may be quite different, while the proclamation of intent from those in charge will certainly evoke different symbols and make different appeals. But there will undoubtedly be a substantial substratum of similar experience, especially in those spheres which involve rationalisation of economic activity, control of investment and consumption, and adjustment of production as between one area and another. If one can obtain an accurate view of how these operations have worked under conditions of coercive integration, light may be thrown on how they would work under more voluntary circumstances. It would, for example, be absurd to make any fundamental distinction between 'noncoercive' and 'coercive' systems of taxation, except in terms of their incidence.

The third reason is that, in the world as it stands, it may be possible to trace the effects of actual attempts at integration by coercion and see whether these have affected contemporary attempts at integration by persuasion. In particular, studies of Hitler's New Order for Europe, and of the Japanese East Asia Co-Prosperity Sphere, may throw light on more recent moves such as those towards the European Community and a Pacific Community. It is true, of course, that the links may be quite tenuous, and that one should be prepared for a nil result in both cases, even for an indication that the earlier coercive schemes actually delayed the implementation of the later ones, because of the resistance they set up. Yet, to the extent that the earlier schemes may have anticipated certain forms of allocation of resources which have since been taken up by other means, or may have led to contacts and arrangements which survived the earlier efforts and remained in being to serve the later ones, much of value can be learnt.

Similarly, there may be much to learn from the experiences of COMECON and the attempts at integration of economies (not, however, of states) in Eastern Europe. If Goodman was right in the view that the

Soviet Union's original intention for conquered states was that they should be incorporated in the Soviet Union itself, on a par with the Ukraine and Byelorussia,[17] then the fact that separate states have continued to exist in Eastern Europe, and have managed to assert a degree of control over their own economies and social conditions, is relevant to an assessment of what can be done by coercion. On the other hand, the absence of overt anti-Soviet movements in the states of Eastern Europe would itself be a relevant factor, especially if it should turn out that people there would not like to see the present degree of integration changed.

Thus, while one would not wish to see integration carried out by force, there may be important evidence in the experience of states subject to attempts at integration by this means, or which are still under domination. It is unfortunate that this kind of investigation lagged behind consideration of voluntary integration, and of the EC in particular, amongst the great majority of theorists.

There is, however, a further criticism which can be made of most integration theorists, and which is particularly apposite to their treatment of France within the context of integration in Western Europe. This relates to the apolitical nature of much of the argument produced in favour of integration. It may seem strange to call it apolitical, since much of it is concerned with elites and pressure-groups, and with the opinions of such ill-defined but potentially significant groups as the young. In fact the complaint is not about the recognition of the groups which do appear in the literature (especially in Haas's influential early work),[18] but about continued miscalculation of their importance and persistence, and the neglect of other interests — less clearly evident, perhaps, but significant none the less — which have been of great influence in Western Europe. At the same time, the concentration of other theorists of the transactionalist school upon unofficial contacts between countries is fascinating and insidious in the attraction it gives to non-political forces and events. A harsh critic might say that integrationists, especially those of the neofunctionalist school, have moved away from politics because its effects too often appear to negate the influence of those cooperating elites who are to be the vehicle of constructive change; again, he might argue that the transactionalists have grasped the undeniable truth that there is unlikely to be voluntary integration between states which have little or no contact, and have shifted it forward to the point at which contacts are so numerous as to negate voluntarism and erect necessity in its place.

Both schools, in fact, depend to a remarkable degree upon the idea of a beneficent necessity which, at some point in human affairs, intervenes in order to overcome the dominance of the sovereign state. There is a loose similarity to Marxism in the implication that quantitative change will lead to qualitative change. Incremental pressure, building up through either increasing transactions or the improved circumstances of elites benefiting from supranational policies, will change political attitudes to the point at which new loyalties appear. The sovereign state, in this kind of formulation, will wither away as it did in the other — not from the same pressures but following a not dissimilar process.

Marxism and integrationism involve a degree of romanticism, in both the formulation of a goal and the identification of those forces which prevent the attainment of the goal in the foreseeable future. The goal itself is simply human happiness, pictured in the Marxist vision as the elimination of coercion through the lifting of class antagonism, and in the integrationist vision as the elimination of endemic war through the adjustment of interests within a supranational framework. In both cases formidable obstacles stand in the way, but they are bound to be overcome in the end. For Marxism the main obstacle has been the multiple forms which capitalism has taken, and its refusal to fit within the categories imposed by Marx and Lenin. For integrationists, the main obstacle has been France, and its refusal to fit within the categories set up in the 1950s.

The French problem will be considered in the next section. For the moment it is sufficient to draw attention to how Joseph Nye attempted to salvage the neo-functionalist case by adding to the kinds of political forces to be taken into account if a realistic analysis were to emerge.[19] Nye pointed out that the impact of President de Gaulle on the process of European integration had led Haas to revise his original formulation of a 'continuous and automatic process leading to political unions', which began essentially with 'integrationist-technocrats and various interest-groups which get governments to create a regional integration organisation'. These groups had remained dominant in Haas's model, until he decided that de Gaulle's activities required the addition of a new sort of participant, the 'actor with "dramatic-political" aims' who could divert the integration process from the predicted course. Nye indicated that people like this were not simply cases of dramatic intervention, but represented quite distinct political styles which could apply in the marketplace, the officers' club or the party office; they could cut across the technocrats, whose style was that of the committee room. In addition, it was necessary to take account of other kinds of actors, such as groups opposed to integration, and mass opinion leaders.

What Nye was showing, in the most charming way, was that the original Haas model was apolitical to the point of unreality. In effect, it had restricted its choice of effective political forces to those which would ensure the success of the operation — would, in other words, guarantee the automaticity of the process which was said to have resulted in the formation of the EEC, and might be repeated wherever these same political forces were found in conjunction. A somewhat similar comment can be made in respect of the incremental process outlined by Deutsch; but this is so much vaguer and more shadowy in operation than Haas's — depending, as it does, upon an indeterminate vista of 'social learning' to create the conditions for political community — that the criticism cannot bite to the same extent.

The main complaint which can be made against integrationist theory, however, is of its neglect of the sovereign state as an institution and actor of major significance. In this sense, much of this book is part of the complaint. The sovereign state is treated by integrationists as inadequate if not despicable, and little is said about its capacities for extension and regeneration; instead, defects in the services it provides for influential groups are seen as opportunities for the creation of supranational bodies. From such a standpoint, the sovereign state is obviously something to be discarded as quickly as possible; yet, as suggested in earlier essays, the power of the state to command loyalties, to provide services and to epitomise the collective demands of its people, has proved to be of very great importance in the three and a half decades since World War II. The integrationist analysis, based upon the immediate postwar decade and confined to Western Europe, is essentially outdated and too narrowly conceived. It takes into account the special circumstances of the major states of Western Europe in a period of catastrophic decline, but not the later experiences of those states, or the experiences of newer states which were unimportant or unconceived when Western Europe was going through its postwar trauma.

Stanley Hoffmann, in a brilliant analysis of how Western Europe was situated in the mid-1960s, has pictured 'a kind of race, between the logic of integration set up by Monnet and analysed by Haas, and the logic of diversity'.[20] As one might expect, the logic of diversity wins, though the kind of diversity represented by President de Gaulle's activities is not accorded an undisputed victory. What Hoffmann calls 'the formidable autonomy of politics' is seen as preserving the nation-state. It is

manifested in the resilience of political systems, the interaction between separate states and a single international system, the role of leaders who believe both in the primacy of 'high politics' over the kind of managerial politics susceptible to functionalism, and in the primacy of the nation, struggling in the world today, over any new form, whose painful establishment might require one's lasting withdrawal from the pressing and exalting daily contest.[21]

There is certainly an autonomy of politics, in the sense that politics is pursued with skills, symbols and tactics that have little or no counterpart elsewhere; but the formidable character of politics arises not so much from its autonomy as from its representativeness, the fact that such a variety of interests can find satisfactory expression within it and can hope to gain. So far as the sovereign state is concerned, this representativeness is heightened by its claims to give its citizens the benefits which will justify its acting on their behalf; politics within the sovereign state leads to the kind of autonomous role which the state then plays on the world stage. In Europe, as we shall see, it is now possible for states to play 'high' and 'low' politics within the structure of the EC and to use that structure for their own purposes elsewhere. This is the very reverse of supra-nationalism as a vital, growing process; instead, it means that the EC enhances the position of the sovereign state, instead of detracting from it.

III

Such an assertion calls for explanation in terms of what has happened to the EC. Let me begin with a brief account of EC history.

All accounts of how the Community began start with the position of the countries of Western Europe after World War II. All except Spain, Switzerland, Sweden and Portugal had been involved in the war and had suffered defeat. Most had been fought over. The Eurocentrism to which their leaders had been accustomed before the war, and to which the rest of the world had conformed, no longer existed. Any significance which Western Europe had was as a long-term prize, to go to either the Russians or the Americans. Britain and France, though treated as victors, were both dependent on American assistance. Furthermore, the Soviet Union took control of Eastern Europe, except for Greece, Turkey and Yugoslavia, and appeared likely to move westwards if circumstances were favourable; its control extended to its own occupied half of Germany, foreshadowing the eventual situation of two states in what had been prewar Germany, and continual fear in the western half that Soviet power would be extended further. This kind of political situation, unparalleled in Europe, was bound to lead to new alignments and arrangements — above all, to a widespread recognition that the states of Western Europe could no longer hope to be at what was called, for a time, 'the top table', when major events were being decided.

New arrangements were also signalled by economic trends. For nearly two centuries Western Europe had been moving towards an effective division of labour between its industrialised areas. The continental railway system, still the most thoroughly integrated in the world (in the sense that trains travel from one country to another with little disturbance of goods and passengers), began prophetically with the Belgian state system which, in 1844, 'was in the form of a cross intersecting at Malines, in which the north-south arms linked with France and Holland, and the east-west arms linked with Germany and the Channel at Ostend, connected with the sea route to Britain'.[22] Railways and waterways, largely constructed in the nineteenth century, still indicate the way in which European industry falls into specialisms and caters for intra-European trade. The problem of the interwar period had been that such specialism and such trade did not expand; the states of Europe concentrated on autarchy and on development of their colonial possessions where those seemed likely to increase metropolitan prosperity. Once World War II was over, and it had become clear that American help was needed, both to provide for rehabilitation of the stricken economies and to defend Western Europe against possible aggression from the Soviet Union, the underlying potential unity of the economies was stressed.

The postwar decline of the sovereign state provided the opportunity for the efforts of Jean Monnet and Maurice Schuman to create supranational institutions which would operate throughout Western Europe. Other factors were also at work — the widespread wish to find means of reconciling France and Germany; the conviction in West Germany that permanent allies must be found, especially the United States; the American determination (alluded to earlier) that 'Europe' must be treated as a whole for both defensive and economic purposes; and the conjunction of Christian Democrat cabinets with Social Democratic parties hostile to communism in West Germany, France and Italy. The supranationalism of the ECSC seemed to make a neat break with Europe's disreputable past, and to introduce new hope. The European regimes, desperate to reconstruct their economies, disturbed by the Soviet threat and racked (in the indispensable case of France) by colonial wars, were receptive to institutions which, backed by the United States, seemed to promise not only a respite from intra-European conflict, but also a viable alternative to the cut-throat economic policies of the interwar years. Others, to whom these possibilities were less attractive, were drawn by the thought that, through some combination of its individual economies, Europe might become a third great power, beholden to neither the United States nor the Soviet Union. Both groups were prepared to accept a certain element of supranationalism in the institutions to be set up — first in the ECSC, established in 1952, then in the EEC — because these would ensure orderliness in the move from traditional protectionism to free trade, and because of the symbolic effect of 'making Europe' through visible institutions which could be said to represent it and nothing else.

It is fair to say, however, that there were special reasons for constructing the EEC (far more important, it has turned out, than the ECSC) in the way in which it eventually emerged. The features of importance, we can see now, were the commitment to a Common Agricultural Policy (CAP) and to assistance to former colonies of member-states. The first ensured that all the original six members of the EEC — France, West Germany, Italy, Belgium, Holland and Luxembourg — had something to offer their farmers; the second lessened the financial load on France's shoulders as it disengaged itself from its African colonies, and facilitated future connections with the new states which appeared in Africa in the 1960s. Thus, in the original plan for the EEC, France, which was one of the two most important members, was guaranteed quite specific advantages. None of the other five was in quite the same position, although there were potential benefits for the Benelux countries in the increased transit trade expected from the agreement, and for Italy in the proposed free movement of labour. However, the second most important member, West Germany, was provided by the EC with a new set of symbols, specifically European in character, which could replace or diminish some of those traditional German symbols which had been tarnished by Hitler and the war; moreover, the construction of a set of European economic institutions alongside the military arrangements of NATO, with the strong backing of the United States, seemed to provide for the Germans further support against the possible menace of the Soviet Union.

There was, in fact, something for everybody in the EEC proposals which were adopted so quickly in the Treaty of Rome in 1957. It was not only governments that were pleased. Supranationalists could lay stress on the relative independence of the EEC Commission. Like the High Authority of the ECSC, which had preceded it, the Commission was given an independent role of initiation and supervision of EC policies, even to the extent of being able to bring member-states before the European Court of Justice if they transgressed the EC's rules. While the

Council of Ministers was to be the supreme rule-making body, the Commission was to be, in significant respects, 'supranational'.

Supranationalists also derived satisfaction from the possibilities of the Economic and Social Committee, which, in the words of the Treaty, was to consist 'of representatives of the various categories of economic and social activity, in particular, representatives of producers, farmers, carriers, workers, dealers, craftsmen, professional occupations and representatives of the general public'. It was the hope of integration theorists that the combination of a disinterested, non-national Commission, and an Economic and Social Committee representing pressure-groups which saw benefits arising from Europe-wide policies rather than narrow national ones, would overcome equally narrow efforts by states to use the EC machinery for sectional advantage.

In terms of policy, the record of the EC since 1957 is of considerable success in removing hindrances to trade within Western Europe, in presenting a common front to other major traders such as the United States and the ASEAN countries, in renewing and expanding the conventions for association with former colonies, and in administering the Common Agricultural Policy, which has become an interest binding together all the members except Britain, which is a net importer of farm products. One should also note that Britain, Ireland and Denmark joined the EC in 1973, that Greece is to do so at the end of 1980 and that Spain and Portugal are expected to join in due course. It is also the case that member-states have become accustomed to working together, or at least consulting together, on major foreign policy questions such as those involving Iran and Afghanistan in 1979-80. A 'Community position' is not unknown at the United Nations and elsewhere in the diplomatic system.

On the other hand, it should be stated that, while the EC has been successful in its negative tasks, such as disposing of the main barriers to intra-European trade, it has not succeeded in establishing any positive policies except the CAP, the Lomé Conventions (which benefit former colonies in Africa, the Caribbean and the Pacific) and the regional policy (intended to assist needy regions within the EC). There is no common policy on transport, energy, currency, investment or taxation. After the long-delayed establishment of direct elections to the European Parliament, the parliament rejected the budget put before it by the Council of Ministers in 1979.

In terms of supranationalism, the EC has gone back, not forward. To some extent this is due to the policies of President de Gaulle. When he returned to office in 1958 he was determined to rid the Commission of the trappings of apparent sovereignty which its most notable chairman, Walter Hallstein, had been concerned to establish. In 1965-66 he imposed what amounted to a unanimity rule upon the Council of Ministers; since then it has become a convention. In spite of seemingly confident statements by integrationists that France would become a 'good member' again when de Gaulle left the scene, his successors Pompidou and Giscard d'Estaing have continued with much the same approach to the EC: it is to be confined to the Treaty of Rome, its major policies will be decided by the Council of Ministers (on which France has an effective veto) and it is to distance itself from American policy while showing a sympathetic understanding in matters which might affect the Atlantic alliance. The 'Gaullist' position has not, however, been confined to France. It cannot be said that any member of the EC has shown a desire to replace national by supranational policy. The smaller members (notably Denmark, Holland and Belgium) have shown a natural desire that 'Community solutions' should be found for major problems, since the alternative is solutions in the interests of major member-states such as France and West Germany; but these 'Community solutions' are essentially compromises between the national interests of the members, and sometimes there are no solutions at all.

The Economic and Social Committee has signally failed to generate that activity amongst European interest-groups which the neo-functionalists had hoped for. It is now a nullity. The body which is of greatest continuing influence within the structure of the EC is the Committee of Permanent Representatives. This consists of diplomats from each of the member-states, available in Brussels all the time, and able to act as a middle term between the Commission and the Council of Ministers. In fulfilling its constitutional task of initiating proposals for the Council to consider, the Commission can test them on the Committee; similarly, members of the Committee can test their approaches on one another, when some major issue is developing inside the EC or in the world at large. For member-states which are unenthusiastic about a particular proposal, but do not want to make a public fuss about it, the Committee provides the means of stating doubts and suggesting changes; it also provides the Commission with a chance to test reactions in private, and to discover whether political opposition will be experienced. The Committee operates at both the diplomatic and the technical level, each of which is provided by the member-states. Its activities mean that the Council of Ministers, when it meets, can confine itself to major matters and to those which have already been tacitly agreed on; but this has not prevented the Council from running into all sorts of difficulties. As the prime political organ of the EC, it is essentially a body in which major interests — those of the member-states — compete for the resources available.

The EC's activities display a constantly changing assessment of national interests by member-states, which calculate what they can get out of the Community's operations, and what should remain within their own control. Although there are cases in which the Commission can call member-states to order if they transgress rules made validly by the Council, the EC's operations represent not the imposition of an overall control, such as the idea of 'integration' implies, but the creation of an extra form of authority from which interests can seek advantage. They can find it, however, only through the sovereign states which are members of the EC, and not by direct access. It is in this sense that the Economic and Social Committee has failed to perform the task allotted to it. Instead of interests organising themselves on a Community-wide scale so as to deal directly with EC bodies, the advantages which the EC has to offer (such as those which arise from the CAP and the regional policy) accrue directly to governments in competition with one another. The clamour aroused by Mrs Thatcher in 1979, to the effect that Britain was paying far more into the EC than it was getting out, was a clear indication of the competitive nature of the EC's processes. It is true that particular interests, such as groups of farmers and particular regions of the member-states, benefit from the EC's activities, but this is not due to their own efforts within the context of the EC. It is the member-state in question which takes the credit. It seems unlikely that the institution of direct elections will change this state of affairs. States will continue to bargain at the Council of Ministers, where national representatives will continue to claim credit for what their countries gain.

This situation is ironically in contrast with federalism as practised in the United States, Australia and Canada. Under a federal system, private interests can go straight to the central government, backed by political parties and local representatives concerned directly with central politics, and can deal with an administration whose electoral chances may be markedly affected by the decisions which are made. These interests do not have to work through the governments of their states or provinces, though assistance from there may be a help; their capacity for bringing pressure to bear on the central authorities can be exercised wholly within the central structure. As the EC has developed, in contrast, the 'provinces' (i.e., the member-states) are all, and the 'centre' (i.e., the Commission) is merely a regulatory and managerial entity, to be thrust aside when serious matters are to be decided. Private interests which approach the Commission will get a sympathetic hearing, but the real lobbying will have to be done amongst departments and politicians in the capitals of the member-states.

It will be seen that forecasts of how the EC would operate were often astray because of an overestimation of the importance to be attached to its allegedly supranational aspects. This in turn arose from an under-estimation of the political forces at work, especially of the role which sovereign states could play as members. Above all, that 'high politics' which Hoffmann refers to — the business of parleying between states on the basis of their existence as separate entities with populations observing loyalties and seeing themselves as citizens of a given state, rather than as butchers or bakers or candlestick-makers — was neglected by observers such as Haas and his followers, while the transactions noted and filed by Deutsch and his men failed to take account of how the individual member-states might be expected to behave. There was, in fact, amongst the integrationists a basic reluctance to take note of historical experience, and an implicit assumption that a new age had begun, one which would contradict and eventually obliterate what had gone before.

This reluctance was especially notable in the case of France, a state which both policy-makers and scholars in the United States tend to underestimate. Many factors may have gone to strengthen this tendency: Americans' incapacity for foreign languages; a sense of outrage that a country so lamentably inadequate in World War II should claim the status of a major power; impatience at the existence of a non-English-speaking culture with widespread influence abroad; sheer incomprehension at the statements of de Gaulle; and perhaps a basic conviction that a country which helped to bring the United States into the world should now defer to its protégé. Whatever the reasons, Americans do habitually downgrade the importance of France, and blame either France or French leaders for conditions which are often more complicated in origin. In the case of the EEC, there was a persistent refusal to recognise that de Gaulle was not exceptional, but was the latest in a long line of French statesmen with similar approaches to international politics. His position — much strengthened by the economic advances France had made before he returned to power in 1958 — was more than personal in application.

It was, in fact, one of the two habitual French positions. Of these, it represented the aspirations of France when strong and in a position to press its claims — aspirations familiar to the French from the efforts of Richelieu, Louis XIV, Napoleon and Clemenceau. The other position — that of France in eclipse, represented, say, by Talleyrand, Guizot and Laval — had been, on the whole, that which France had displayed during the decade after World War II, during which the position may well have been mistaken by observers for a permanent attitude. It was, however, a position which, in the past, France had assumed of necessity, only to cast it aside when opportunity arose. So it was when de Gaulle came to office; and it is not surprising that his successors should have followed his example, since France is still economically strong, is militarily significant, and has repaired the breaches in its ex-colonial relationships. Not to recognise the likelihood of this evolution was to make nonsense of the idea of effective political analysis.

The defects of the integrationist position in respect of the EC can be summed up as: a disinclination to give sufficient weight to traditional political interests; an overplaying of the common interests of European states, and a neglect of the range of quite specific, historically unique, and often negative, interests which drew them together in the 1950s; far too much emphasis on the degree of autonomy which centralised 'supra-national' institutions would be allowed to exercise once the states of Western Europe had returned to something like a normal economic condition; a similar overemphasis on the extent and effectiveness of 'European' sentiment, and on the likelihood of its growth; and, in general, a neglect of the capacity of the sovereign state to satisfy the interests to be found amongst its citizens. To a startling extent, the integrationist movement was a case of wishful thinking, so far as Western Europe was concerned.

IV

If the theorists of integration are to be regarded as having significance beyond the context of the EC, some observations about other cases of possible integration are in order. It should be noted that the pioneers of the movement were cautious about extension beyond Europe, but that many of their followers showed no such restraint. 'In their longing for successful integration, and hence peace, many academics have easily slipped into the position of seeing Europe not as an exception to the course of history and the near-universal persistence of nationalism, but as a harbinger of the future and as a model for others to emulate.'[23] Yet, in fact, the world has seen in the past three decades a remarkable degree of 'autonomy-seeking behaviour'.[24] This has occurred in existing political units, as well as being manifested in the great increase in the number of sovereign states which has followed decolonisation. Various imperial schemes for retaining former arrangements and preventing the appearance of a number of separate states (such as the Federation of the West

Indies, the original French schemes for West and Equatorial Africa, and the East African Community) have failed, leaving behind something which critics often call 'balkanisation', but which, in the cases in question, appears to satisfy the citizens and politicians concerned. In addition, there have been attempts to escape from existing conglomerate states (successful in the case of Bangladesh, unsuccessful in that of Biafra), rumblings of discontent in Eastern Europe, and disruptive pressures from Basques and Quebeckers. If there is a trend towards integration, such as Etzioni postulated, it has been well concealed.

It is clear that, throughout the world, there have been movements for smaller, 'national' states, especially in post-colonial situations. These urges have usually been satisfied by the setting up of sovereign states, which, even when allegedly not 'viable' (a word for which there are as many meanings as users), resist incorporation in larger groupings. Such autonomy-seeking behaviour does not preclude forms of cooperation between the states in question, though it is noticeable that the effect of closer contact and more transactions of certain kinds with neighbouring states may be to engender resistance to further cooperation; there is certainly no evidence that it leads inexorably to incorporation, integration, or even to institutions of cooperation.[25]

The cases of restless, disruptive provinces (as with Quebec and Biafra) may be satisfied by rearrangement of functions within the overall institutions of a particular sovereign state; but if there is an irreconcilable conflict, and circumstances are favourable to a break (as they were in Singapore and Bangladesh, though in quite different ways), the only solution may be secession and the formation of a quite new state. It is noticeable, however, that, while a number of schemes for the integration of existing colonial units have fallen apart (the Federation of the West Indies being the outstanding one), those which have converted existing colonial units into sovereign states have normally been successful, even in cases in which communal rivalry was intense and there were doubts about whether the new state could hold together. The lesson here seems to be that if the potential structure of a sovereign state is already present in the shape of a working colonial administration (carrying with it many of the benefits to citizens, in the form of provision, which are characteristic of the sovereign state), it is easier to sustain the state after independence than if a new structure has been cobbled together to promote 'viability'. If the constituent units of such a structure have not been accustomed to work together under the colonial regime, they may not do so afterwards.

It might be said further of the presence or absence of integrative forces in the postwar world that we do not have any recent cases of federalism to compare with either the 'classic' federations (the USA, Switzerland, Canada and Australia) or those created in conditions of postwar occupation or decolonisation (e.g., West Germany, India and Malaysia); and that there is no case of states voluntarily copying the 'supranationalism' of the EC though it is nearly thirty years since the ECSC came into being.

V

What, then, is left of the theory of integration? The obvious conclusion is that, although one should not claim that sovereign states cannot cooperate, or cannot link themselves closely for particular purposes, there is empirical support for the view that sovereign states remain the dynamic elements in world affairs. The sovereign state is not worn out, and it is more popular than ever, in the sense that efforts are still being made to form sovereign states, rather than to amalgamate them. Integration, however defined, is in no sense impossible; but it is unlikely, and seems to be getting more so.

At all events, it can also be asserted that neither an increase in transactions nor the establishment of allegedly supranational institutions causes integration. After nearly thirty years of experience of both these influences, Western Europe remains itself, but also its separate selves. To a startling extent, the impact of EC membership is unnoticeable. The countries of Western Europe look, sound, and act as if they were still separate. There is no sense in passing from France to Switzerland, or West Germany to Austria, or Britain to Sweden, that one is moving from a Community member to a state that is not one. It is true that the governments and businessmen of the member-states are aware of the EC, and that their farmers have seized what they could get from the CAP; but the governments operate as if they were engaged in normal international politics, rather than in that special kind of relationship which Monnet and his fellows envisaged. The wartime and immediate postwar revulsion against the sovereign state has spent itself. In NATO the same is true. National forces remain national, and negotiation continues to be in terms of national interest, in spite of the unifying influence of the shared desire to keep the USA involved in European affairs.

Notes

1. Theodore H. White, *Fire in the Ashes: Europe in Mid-Century* (New York, 1953), p. 272.

2. See, e.g., E.H. Carr, *The Future of Nations* (London, 1941 and *Conditions of Peace* (London, 1942), and W. Friedmann, *The Crisis of the National State* (London, 1943). David Mitrany's writings, collected in *The Functional Theory of Politics* (London, 1975), are also relevant.

3. Amitai Etzioni, *The Hard Way to Peace* (New York, 1962), p. 177.

4. By now there are special problems of nomenclature in respect of 'Europe', arising from the fact that the European Coal and Steel Community (ECSC) was established first, that this was followed by the European Economic Community (EEC) and Euratom, and that later the institutions of the three were amalgamated. They form a single European Community (EC) of which the EEC is clearly the vital element. Unless it is necessary to refer to one of the three directly, I shall use the term European Community to describe the institutions at large. The EC Commission seems to use 'Communities' and 'Community' indifferently.

5. Charles Pentland, *International Theory and European Integration* (New York, 1973) p. 18.

6. Ernst B. Haas, 'The Study of Regional Integration: Reflections on the Joy and Anguish of Pretheorising', *International Organisation*, vol. XXIV, no. 4, August 1970, p. 607.

7. I have vivid recollections of a class of American graduate students in 1962, who were appalled when told that 'Europe' would be most unlikely to federate as the USA had done; that the 'supranational' powers of the European Commission would be increasingly circumscribed; and that the behaviour of France was due to something more than the personality of President de Gaulle.

8. Bruce Russett, *Power and Community in World Politics* (San Francisco, 1974), pp. 325-9.

9. Ibid., p. 329.

10. Donald James Puchala, *International Politics Today* (New York, 1971), p. 121.

11. Karl W. Deutsch, *The Analysis of International Relations* (Englewood Cliffs, NJ, 1968), p. 159.

12. Ibid., p. 160.

13. Ernst B. Haas, 'International Integration: The European and the Universal Process', in Karl W. Deutsch *et al.*, *International Political Communities* (Garden City, 1966), p. 94 (originally published in *International Organisation*, vol. XV, no. 4, Autumn 1961).

14. Haas, 'The Study of Regional Integration', p. 610.

15. The significance of pace is well brought out in Peter J. Katzenstein, 'Hare and Tortoise: The Race Toward Integration', *International Organisation*, vol. XXV, no. 2, Spring 1971.

16. Puchala, *International Politics Today*, p. 122.

17. Elliot R. Goodman, *The Soviet Design for a World State* (New York, 1960).

18. Ernst B. Haas, *The Uniting of Europe: Political, Social and Economical Forces 1950-1957* (London, 1958).

19. J.S. Nye, 'Comparing Common Markets: A Revised Neo-Functionalist Model', *International Organisation*, vol. XXIV, no. 4, Autumn 1970, esp. pp. 799-803.

20. 'Obstinate or Obsolete? The Fate of the Nation-State and the Case of Western Europe', in Stanley Hoffmann (ed.), *Conditions of World Order* (Boston, 1968), pp. 129 ff.

21. Ibid., p. 149.

22. Sidney Pollard, *European Economic Integration 1815-1970* (London, 1974), p. 43.

23. This quotation is from K.J. Holsti, 'Change in the International System: Interdependence, Integration and Fragmentation', in Ole R. Holsti, Randolph M. Sivisson and

Alexander George (eds.), *International System Change* (Boulder, Colorado, 1980). I had the privilege of seeing this article before publication.

24. Ibid.

25. Holsti (ibid.) is especially telling in his account of how the American-Canadian relationship has engendered forms of resistance; much the same could be said of the American-Mexican and Australian-New Zealand relationships.

6 THE ECONOMIC WORLD AND THE POLITICAL WORLD

There are both an economic world and a political world. The symbols of the first include international bankers, ships disgorging cargo, funds being moved from one country to another, multinational corporations and crises in the balance of payments. Amongst symbols of the second are military forces and their weapons, summit meetings of leaders, meetings of the UN and diplomatic couriers. Clearly, they differ in nature and emphasis, and in the kind of knowledge needed to understand them; a question that arises in practice is whether we can understand both, and whether they are linked with one another or can be regarded as distinct for purposes of study and policy.

Since Adam Smith, efforts have been made by economists to disentangle the economic and political worlds, and treat the economic world as autonomous. In Smith's case, it was because he was in revolt against conventional mercantilist beliefs which stressed the need for state action to direct trade in what was said to be the national interest, but which, in his view, inhibited trade and reduced national wealth. What to Smith was an urgent matter of policy has become, amongst his successors, something of a morality:

> Whatever his particular perspective, the international economist is chiefly concerned with individuals. Like other economists, he is an intellectual descendent of Adam Smith and of the nineteenth-century Utilitarians, and though he may for analytical purposes treat the nation as a single unit, he is not likely to regard it as the end in view.[1]

Yet, treating the nation as the end in view is, to a large extent, what happens in the political world; and students of international politics, like economists, have tended to stick to their own view of what is important in world affairs, and to maintain, in effect, a separation between world economics and that part of the world's affairs which concerns peace and war and has been widely designated 'political'. It is rare to find efforts to bring the two together.[2]

Yet we have to try to do so, just as we have to try to bring domestic and international politics together — because the same bodies and the same persons are involved in both. In the economic world, it is expected that states will have policies on trade, currency and investment, and that they will attempt to put these into effect. Whether economists think in terms of individuals or not, individuals appear to think in terms of the state in which they live, and the prosperity or otherwise which that state succeeds in obtaining within the international economy. The same cabinet will have to consider external economic policy, domestic economic policy and what is normally called 'foreign' policy. In practice, the official external behaviour of the state will be affected by influences from all three of these. From a politician's standpoint, there is no difference in substance between a decision on trade policy and one on alliance policy; they must, as far as possible, be adjusted to one another, but the sources from which they come are pressures from domestic and foreign interests, and will be responded to in similar ways. There are genuine problems, however, in seeing how the economic and political worlds fit together.

I

Let me begin by asking what any state's external economic policy involves. It is convenient to divide the states of the world into three categories, since this is how they are normally divided at international discussions, such as those on a New International Economic Order (NIEO) — the rich, western, industrialised countries (those of North America, Western Europe, Japan, Australia and New Zealand); those in Eastern Europe,' members of COMECON; and those of the Third World, the poor non-industrialised countries. This division is conventional rather than scientific, since it ignores the considerable wealth of various countries in Latin America and the Middle East, the growing industrialisation of some countries in East Asia such as the Koreas and the situation of China, Vietnam and South Africa. However, it will do for the purposes of this essay.

Taking the rich countries first, there are certain things which any policy is likely to aim at. These include a sound balance of payments; opportunities for foreign investment on reasonable terms which preclude confiscation by foreign governments; access to sources of foreign investment, if, as in Canada and Australia, there are still natural resources to be exploited; an exchange rate that facilitates exports, or, at least, does not hinder them; dependable sources of raw materials; reliable and expanding markets; and, in general, an external position which promotes domestic employment but does not encourage inflation.

Not all of these aims are likely to prove compatible (in particular, the last may be impossible and may conflict with some of the others), but they are widely advocated in the rich countries. Basically, they represent the requirements of *'status quo'* powers, those which are broadly satisfied with the shape of the international economy and do not wish to alter it, but wish to benefit as much as possible from its existing arrangements.

If we turn to the communist states of Eastern Europe, excluding Albania and including the Soviet Union, very much the same list of aims can be drawn up. As put in official propaganda, it will probably be coloured by statements about the intrigues of imperialism and the lasting friendship between the socialist countries and those of the Third World, but it will come to much the same in the end. This is because the Eastern European countries are, to a considerable extent, also *'status quo'* powers. Some of them (East Germany, Czechoslovakia, Poland) are highly industrialised and have much the same balance between agriculture and manufactures as their counterparts in Western Europe, with similar problems of balancing benefits domestically between these two economic sectors, and of organising fruitful trade with neighbours. Others (Bulgaria, Hungary and Romania) are more rural in character and need to ensure profitable exports of commodities in order to maintain their standards of living. In each case they are countries with relatively little to learn in technological terms, compared with the countries of the Third World. They see their external opportunities as largely a matter of exchange with other industrialised countries, whether socialist or capitalist. They do not have the same public need as the rich countries for sources of investment, favourable exchange rates and sources of raw materials, since the cooperation of socialist countries within COMECON is supposed to take care of all of these; but the competition for such resources is continued in COMECON in directly political terms, and is intended to attain the same objectives as the rich countries may achieve by economic competition. Industrialised countries have much the same external economic objectives, whatever their political labels.

The aims of the poor countries, on the other hand, correspond to their earlier stages of economic development, and to their strongly stated wish for rapidly advancing standards of living. They are not *'status quo'* powers, but wish for a change in the *status quo*. In some cases they share an objective with the first two groups of countries, such as a sound balance of payments; but in their case this will be linked with the demand for a bigger role for international organisations, so that countries in balance of payments difficulties can obtain short- and long-term help in maintaining their liquidity, and can get it without having to pay market prices to the international banking system. They too, like the Canadas and Australias, will want foreign investment to develop unexploited natural resources, but will put more stress on conditions of investment that limit the repatriation of profits, and give considerable say to host governments in deciding how far the investment should go.[3] They will actively seek foreign aid for development, laying their emphasis on the needs which arise from economic backwardness — improvement of infrastructure in education, transport, sources of power, etc.; the transfer of technology; and the promotion of industrial growth — but also upon aid which will foster self-reliance. They will stress multilateralism in aid, rather than bilateralism. So far as their exports of raw materials and food are concerned, they will look for international action to provide for prices which do not fall but continue to rise so that their terms of trade are not worsened; and they will hope for exchange rates which neither deter foreign investors nor accentuate their own balance of payments difficulties. They will press for preferential markets in the rich countries for their manufactured goods, and for access which enables them to compete with local products. In such new areas of economic diplomacy as the law of the sea, and the protection of the environment, their emphasis will lie on compensation for alleged past abuses, and on their own control of resources which may previously have been regarded as available to any state which could exploit them.

These aims are less market-oriented than the aims of the rich countries, and call for more in the way of official international action (i.e., multilateral activity by international organisations) than either the rich western countries or those of Eastern Europe require. A hasty judgement would say that Third-World aims are more 'political' than those of the western countries, which would be styled more 'economic'. Yet this would be a facile conclusion. A *status quo* position can be just as 'political' as one which looks for change, a Metternich as active in politics as a Napoleon; the essence of a *status quo* position is that there is something to defend, and that the interests involved will go to considerable lengths to see that change does not cause them disadvantage. So far as international measures are concerned, the rich states of the west have been active, first in setting up institutions which would keep the position as they wanted it (institutions such as GATT and the International Monetary Fund (IMF)), and then, under disturbed conditions, finding new ways of managing the international monetary system so as to prevent their own loss. Susan Strange describes the efforts of the 'managing oligarchy of states' in the 1960s, which involved

> the international cooperation practised by national central banks and
> most often undertaken for the collective management of crises that
> arose, not between states, but when international financial and money
> markets became threateningly nervous and unstable. The purpose
> was not so much to make up for a non-existent international monetary
> order, substituting the Fund's rule-book for a world central bank, as
> actually to simulate such a bank. By acting together — even if only at
> times of crisis — the central banks of the affluent countries were trying
> in the 1960s to impose, on behalf of public authority and in the general
> public interest, some order and restraint over the more unruly and
> disorderly activities of private enterprise; or, if this were impossible,
> at least to cancel them out . . .
>
> In this plot, the chief actors were states but to the extent that their
> opponents were financial markets, those markets must also be counted
> as actors — though perhaps like gods, angels, devils and fairies in
> fiction-drama, actors of a different order from mortals. If they did not
> speak, they still mimed their lines most effectively by means of price
> movements and the shifting of funds. In this plot, the lines for states
> were spoken by Governors of central banks and their officials; and the
> focus of the historical perspective for this kind of international
> cooperation is more on the 1920s and 1930s than on the 1950s.[4]

Such an example illustrates not only the interest of sovereign states in
monetary order, but also their capacity to create new institutions of order
(i.e., 'authorities' as described in Essay 1) so as to have a political framework in which to protect their interests.

A further aspect of the external economic policies of both rich and poor
states is their common tendency to use tariffs, quotas and other protectionist devices when it appears that domestic difficulties will arise from
unrestricted imports. Free trade is, to a large extent, an economists'
construct, an aspiration which economists have pursued since their
discipline began with Adam Smith, and which was dignified in the mid-
nineteenth century in Britain by public debates in which the terms 'free
trade' and 'political economy' were often used indiscriminately. It is
much less of a political reality. The states which now seem most anxious
to press free-trade policies on others — West Germany, Japan, the United
States — gained much of their industrial strength during protectionist
periods in which goods from foreign countries were excluded when they
interfered with the growth of infant industries or with powerful interests

aiming at internal consolidation of firms, and the rationalisation of local industries. Furthermore, all rich countries are likely to impose or retain protection when local interests demand such action. Textiles, clothing and footwear are highly sensitive industries where Third-World imports are concerned, and the United States, Japan and the members of the European Community retain controls on imports of temperate-zone foodstuffs which might compete successfully with what their own farmers produce. Free trade is a policy for the economic upswing, when both imports and domestic products can be comfortably absorbed by a rising domestic market. When the upswing stops, protectionist urges make themselves felt as active interests within the domestic political system.

It is thus foolish to think of international economics as something essentially apolitical, which can be effectively studied without taking politics into account. It is also foolish to think that, because some actions in foreign policy look more 'political' than others, the economic actions can be neglected. Whether one is concerned with rich or poor countries, the economic and political worlds cannot be separated.

II

The two are not separate in origin. Both derive from scarcity, whether that is seen as absolute (in conditions of near-hunger) or as relative (in conditions such as those of industrialised countries, in which scarcity operates in the process of choice within the enormous range of consumer goods available). In economics, the price mechanism (coupled, in the case of the command economies of the communist countries, with systems of rationing and formal allocation) decides, in terms of supply and demand, who gets what, when, and how. In politics, pressures in the search for advantage operate so as to distribute whatever the authorities have to grant, or whatever they can provide access to. In each case there are scarce goods, heavy demands, and a process of allocation which decides whose claims will be met. The 'goods', which in the economic sense are most readily seen as tangible objects, may in both the economic and political spheres be services, and even such intangibles as prestige and status.

While the two are separate in origin, there is a sort of primacy to economics, in the sense that providing oneself with food, clothes and shelter is prior to other activities, and has to be attended to, by both individuals and communities, before they can concentrate on other things. Nevertheless, there is also a sort of primacy to politics. Robinson

Crusoe on his island did not need to engage in politics when he was by himself; he concentrated on growing and making things. Once Man Friday arrived, however, Crusoe needed a structure of authority with himself on top, a point which is further emphasised in the story when he has to deal with the pirates, who form an extraneous interest attempting to overthrow the structure he has created. At this stage he moves, as it were, from domestic to international politics. Crusoe represents the primitive politics of domination as well as the primitive economics of subsistence. For him, as for any contemporary state's government, the actions needed for economic and political ends are not contradictory, and would be hard to separate.

In practice, neither economics nor politics is likely to appear in a 'pure' form to any state; once again, scarcity is the reason. No state is able to command the resources which will satisfy all the wants of its people. In consequence, the 'pure' market process involving free choice, free supply, free movement of prices and of factors of production, is interfered with by state intervention directed towards the advantage of various interests which have gained priority. In this sense, a political element is inevitable in economics. Similarly, in the politics of any state no amount of pressure, however well organised, can produce resources which are unavailable because of deficiencies in the state's natural endowment or because of an acutely adverse balance of payments.

We are thus justified in regarding the economic and political worlds as mingling at a great many points, whether our focus is on the individual state or on the whole world. It is possible to separate the two for purposes of analysis, but not to exorcise one from the other. There are numerous disquisitions on 'pure economics', and perhaps there could be the same on 'pure politics', which presumably would be concerned solely with contests for supremacy; internationally, it would be what Stanley Hoffmann and others call 'high politics'. In either case, however, reality is a mixture; and theory must always return to reality in the end.

III

In one's preoccupation with the attempts of professional students of economics and politics to put some distance between their worlds, it is advisable to remember that influential schools of thought — and, often, the man in the street — have been convinced for a long time that separation of the two is unrealistic, because the reality of international politics is domination by economic interests through force and fraud.

To illustrate this point of view, one can take Evelyn Waugh's marvellous novel *Scoop*, and its character Mr Baldwin (a name with more significance in 1938 than now), a mighty financier who has a Costa Rican passport, but declares himself a Briton and 'sighs for the days of Pam and Dizzy'. In some respects akin to Somerset Maugham's Hairless Mexican in *Ashenden*, he explains his activities in Ishmaelia, a mythical African republic uncomfortably close to those of the present day, but modelled on Ethiopia and Liberia:

> It is all very simple. There has been competition for the mineral rights of Ishmaelia, which, I may say as their owner, have been preposterously over-valued. In particular the German and Russian Governments were willing to pay extravagantly — but in kind. Unhappily for them the commodities they had to offer — treasures from the Imperial palaces, timber, toys and so forth — were not much in demand in Ishmaelia — in presidential circles at any rate. President Jackson had long wanted to make adequate provision for his retirement, and I was fortunately placed in being able to offer him gold for his gold concession, and my rivals found themselves faced by the alternative of abandoning their ambitions or upsetting President Jackson. They both preferred the latter, more romantic course. The Germans, with a minimum of discernment, chose to set up a native of low character named Smiles as prospective dictator. I never had any serious fears of him. The Russians, more astutely, purchased the Young Ishmaelite party and are, as you see, momentarily in the ascendant . . .
>
> You should ask me whether I have any message for the British public. I have. It is this: *Might must find a way*. Not '*Force*', remember; other nations use force; we Britons alone use 'Might'. Only one thing can set things right — sudden or extreme violence, or, better still, the effective threat of it.[5]

The Costa Rican Mr Baldwin, who knows that, if the British public is told to compare him with Cecil Rhodes and T.E. Lawrence, it will warm to him, is Waugh's ironic depiction of radical conceptions of imperialism in the 1930s. Fed from liberal sources, especially J.A. Hobson's *Imperialism*, and more recently by Lenin's work of the same name, which characterised imperialism as 'the highest stage of capitalism', these conceptions contained two elements. One was moral indignation at the way in which profit-seeking swashbucklers had seized land, oil, gold and diamonds in backward areas, and forced the British, French and other governments to act in their favour by setting up colonial administrations.

The other was intellectual conviction that there was something inevitable about these efforts. Capitalism would fail unless it expanded into areas with raw materials and markets, and capitalist states would intrigue against one another to the point of war, in order to get what they wanted.[6]

Since the 1930s this radical analysis has been given further currency by Third-World countries eager to justify their demands for concessions through UNCTAD, and their advocacy of an NIEO. While the Mr Baldwins are no longer discussed at length, the analysis of the past remains much the same: capitalism despoiled the colonial areas for its own purposes, removing their assets and leaving behind social disruption and economic deprivation. The moral indignation is expressed in the demand that capitalism now pay for its past misdeeds. If this way of looking at the world is adopted, there is no difficulty about arriving at a basic judgement on the relations between the economic and political worlds; the rich prey on the poor to their own advantage. In more sophisticated variations, such as the contemporary 'centre-periphery' and 'dependencia' schools, [7] the rich need not *mean* to oppress the poor; they cannot help themselves. In either case, economics triumphs. The political world is the handmaiden of the economic.

There has always been something dramatic about the radical approach to international politics, and it is not surprising that in its present-day forms it still excites the young. However, this does not make it a satisfactory explanation of how the economic and political worlds connect with one another. It is not good, for example, at explaining the relations of rich countries with one another; yet the rich countries' trade and investment are primarily with one another, and their major profits appear to derive from this. Their economic connections with Third-World countries are significant when aggregated, but still occupy second place to their mutual connections. Nor are they engaged in cut-throat competition with one another to the extent that earlier analyses suggested.[8] The rich states are largely concerned with the condition of their own domestic markets; they then concern themselves with trade with other rich states; and their concern with Third-World states is much more in terms of essential raw materials — which they now buy, rather than own or steal — and much less in markets. The connection between the rich countries as a whole, and the poor countries as a whole, does not appear to have the quality of necessity, or to involve continuously the vital interests of the rich countries, except in such situations as the OPEC control over oil prices. Instead, there is a largely incidental quality to the relationship. Klaus Knorr makes a useful distinction between economic *dominance* and economic *domination*, which helps to highlight much of the current rich-poor connection:

> Both relationships are characterised by unequal economic constraints. If the constraint is produced involuntarily, it indicates economic dominance; if it is deliberate, it indicates economic domination. Beyond doubt, the massive weight of the American economy in the world gives it dominance. But most events in the American economy, whether planned or unplanned, take place without any intent to impose their repercussions on other economies. Such effects are incidental. Similarly, economic dominance may reflect superior economic innovation that is not cultivated, at least primarily, to cause adjustments in other economies. Countries do not contract economic depression or inflation, and governments do not ordinarily foster economic growth, in order to benefit or hurt other countries.[9]

Of course, whether one suffers dominance or domination, one is still in an inferior position; and this helps to explain why so much Third-World publicity is so vehement, not simply in stressing that inferiority, but in claiming that it is due to domination.

The economic world, when viewed as a whole, is rather as follows. The rich countries trade and invest very heavily with one another. They also trade with and invest in the poor countries, but not to the same extent. This particular combination of trade and investment can be explained partly in terms of the need for raw materials (e.g., Japan's need for such imports), partly in terms of the advantage to be gained from investing in labour-intensive industry in low-wage countries (e.g., Japanese and American investment in parts of East Asia and Latin America), partly in terms of long-established relationships dating from colonial times (e.g., much of France's economic activity in Africa), and partly in terms of growing trade and investment with the oil-producing countries, Korea and Malaysia. In some cases, notably in East Asia, it has led to substantial domestic development by poor countries. Mostly, however, it has not had much effect. Poor countries continue to be poor, and the gap between their standards of living and those of the rich countries continues to widen.

This gap, normally calculated in terms of GNP per head, is not so wide between the elites of the rich and poor countries as between the non-elites, who live well in most of the rich countries and very badly in the poor ones. Efforts are made by the poor countries, acting together, to reduce the gap by diplomatic means (they also attempt to reduce it individually through bilateral negotiations with rich countries). These diplomatic efforts centre on the demand at the UN for an NIEO, but are also pursued in attempts to set up cartels of raw material producers such as OPEC. On the whole, however, the world economy proceeds in much the same way, in spite of debates at the UN, which may produce some result because of their protracted nature, and because of the wish of the rich countries of the West not to quarrel too violently with many of the poor countries, but will not produce much. In the main, the economic 'clout' of the rich countries is so great — in their skill and technical proficiency, their innovation of new processes, their capital resources and their marketing capacities, and in their own substantial buying power — that they can expect to be in a state of dominance, and to exercise some domination, for a long time to come. The states of Eastern Europe, with their command economies, still lack sufficient 'clout' of the same kind to make more than an occasional impact on the condition of the poor countries.

IV

In the preceding paragraph, some mention has been made of attempts by poor countries to use the UN to obtain concessions from the rich. This is one way in which the political world intrudes upon the economic world.

The poor countries' effort through UNCTAD, the UN General Assembly and the specialised agencies, to effect major transfers of resources from the rich as a matter of course, rather than as a result of intermittent and unpredictable aid, is pursued with great energy but indifferent success. In 1979, for example, this effort was to have reached something of a peak: there were to be special UN conferences on trade, technology and land reform; lengthy GATT talks on trade liberalisation were to be completed; it was also hoped that there would be further progress towards a common fund for commodities and common rights to the seabed. None of these made the progress which the Group of 77 sought;[10] indeed, it boycotted the signing of the GATT agreements. At the same time, rifts were apparent amongst the 'poor' countries through the presence of states which were becoming uncomfortably rich, especially the oil producers (which by 1979 had become substantial aid-givers in their own right) and East Asian states such as Singapore and Malaysia.

The rich countries had, on the whole, stuck together in requesting modifications of the schemes for discussion (notably the common fund), and in retaining in the face of Third-World protests the understandings arrived at in the GATT talks. To a large extent, the objections of the rich countries to schemes such as the original common fund proposal were based upon the distortions which these would introduce into the market process (e.g., permanently high prices for raw materials), and the role proposed for the poor countries in operating the schemes. Basically, the objection was to automatic transfers of resources from rich to poor.

At the same time, the rich countries were using another set of international organisations to deal with the matters affecting them directly, and the poor countries at a further remove. In GATT, the OECD and the IMF they discussed their mutual trading relations and the barriers between them; they compared their exchange rate policies, their attitude to gold and the special drawing rights issued by the IMF; they also took account of one another's policies in foreign aid. Although their mutual negotiations were kept quieter than the declamatory approach of the Group of 77, occasional rifts appeared between them, e.g., between the EEC states and others over the disposal of agricultural supluses. The rich states, which conduct a kind of rearguard diplomacy at the UN when Group of 77 demands have to be answered, also conduct a mutual diplomacy about what is good behaviour for rich countries in the present world. Much the same can presumably be said of diplomacy within COMECON. In all three instances — Group of 77, rich states of the West, and Eastern European communist states — attempts are made at protecting individual states' interests while retaining some consensus on major issues.

Thus, we can see a variety of political processes taking place in a number of settings, each of them directed towards economic ends. In terms of the categories used in Essay 1, the interests are there in search of advantage; who or what can be designated as the authorities? Is 'government' a visible factor?

As suggested in Essay 1, it is mostly pointless to look for a determinate sovereign in international politics, although at times one may see the great powers of the moment playing this role in certain respects. In recent times the United States has played it in regard to currency arrangements amongst the rich states (certainly in the setting up, and the management for many years, of the IMF); and at meetings of the OECD the opinions of the USA normally carry great weight. Sometimes, the United States's authority in NATO spills over into its economic discussions with the states of Western Europe. Similarly, and indeed more directly, the Soviet Union plays the role of a sovereign in COMECON, though no longer that of an absolute ruler.

In addition, however, it was suggested that, when consensus is achieved within the international system, it operates as a form of authority which enables the agreement to be sustained. This is how international law, of the kind represented by the Vienna Convention on diplomatic rights, is made and kept. In the economic sphere, the interests represented at Law of the Sea conferences by the participating states have arrived at consensus about a 200-mile economic zone for each coastal state, and this too is becoming law. The agreements which states come to are signalised by the specialised agencies instructed to administer them, such as the IMF and ICAO. These bodies represent, in the most rudimentary way, authorities on a world scale; but they remain so, only so long as the mass of states continues to support them. Some, such as UNCTAD, have not achieved this sort of consensus, and so have nothing much to administer.

It is unlikely that there will be any great advance from this rudimentary position. One cannot look forward to an enlargement of economic agencies to the point at which the world economy becomes subject to collective control in all or most of its aspects. The areas in which international authorities have been established — such as posts and telecommunications, meteorology, civil aviation and navigation — are characterised by the need for some minimum observance of common rules if there is to be any effective intercourse at all between states. Beyond that minimum (in such areas as civil aviation, for example) there is resistance to any extension of authority; and in the case of exchange rates, stabilised for so long by the IMF, there was what amounted to a rejection of the whole system when the US dollar became inconvertible in 1971.

The root of the matter is that livelihoods and the level of employment are vital domestic issues in every state. No state will allow these to be determined by an external body, unless there are compensating advantages of unquestionable value, or unless the state is subject to irresistible compulsion. State sovereignty is at its testing point in the economic world, because of the conviction of every government that its people will disown it unless it strives to retain control of the domestic economy, and meet the economic demands most fervently expressed. Bread riots are amongst the oldest and most basic forms of protest. To governments, it is essential to provide the appearance of economic control. The political world is alive with extravagant economic claims by governments about what they will do, and what they will prevent.

Yet these economic claims, like so many made in respect of foreign policy, are subject to severe limitations; the very nature of the economic world provides an abundance of these. Some will be expressed in directly political terms (e.g., no amount of rhetoric will provide further foreign investment for a state which nationalises foreign corporations without compensating their owners, or persistently repudiates the interest payments on foreign debts), but most will arise from the operations of the international economy itself. If too much sugar or copper or wheat is being produced, it will not be sold. If manufactured goods from a particular state price themselves out of the market, they will not be sold either. If balance of payments deficits occur year after year, loans to finance them will cease, though some great power may step in to help because of its non-economic interest. However much states may emphasise their sovereignty, they must bow to economic realities like these. The distribution throughout the world of wealth and resources involves facts which cannot be gainsaid by individual states, unless they are very powerful and are prepared to devote years of effort to changing the situation.

The inexorable quality of basic economic facts may, in itself, create opportunities for states to influence one another's policies. Resources are needed for any enterprise. If they are unavailable locally (as is often the case with Third-World states), they will have to be obtained from other states. They will not normally be made available from foreign sources unless the enterprise seems likely to be successful in economic terms — or unless the foreign sources seek to create a position of dependence which will give them domination over the state requiring them. Sometimes, as a matter of policy, this sort of dependence is deliberately created by major powers in order to give them leverage over other states' policies. The Soviet Union and China may import commodities in quantities which do not make economic sense from countries which they wish to influence; similarly, they may invest in projects such as steel works in India and the TanZam railway in Africa. These attempts at creating dependence are not always successful. The Soviet Union seems to have achieved success in respect of Cuba, but has not done well with other states such as Egypt and Indonesia. As with any other attempt to politicise the economic world in a thorough, long-lasting fashion, the search for a position of dominance which is not warranted by economic considerations is likely to be costly and prolonged.

V

The point just made is apposite to a question which arises whenever hostility between states becomes apparent, and especially when it is linked with the politics of alliances. It is whether hostility should be expressed in economic terms, by cessation of trade and other forms of economic connection, or confined to diplomatic representations, inimical statements, symbolic military movements and the strengthening of alliance connections. The problem can be especially acute for small and medium powers, notably producers of foodstuffs and raw materials like Canada, Australia and New Zealand. It can also be significant for major exporters of manufactures like West Germany (in relation to East Germany and other states in Eastern Europe) and Japan (in respect of China and the eastern areas of the Soviet Union). In all these cases, allies of the United States have been asked at times to show economic hostility towards the Soviet Union and China, and in so doing to restrict existing trade and to prejudice future opportunities. Similar problems arose over the hostage crisis in Iran in 1980.

The problem expresses itself as a conflict of interests. On the one hand, the state in question wishes to retain its alliance with the United States. On the other, it must take account of the interests of its farmers, manufacturers and traders. It must also try to calculate the effect of the trade sanctions upon the adversary, the likely duration of the crisis or period of acute hostility, the possibility that states less closely associated with its own ally will seize the market in the state which is to suffer sanctions, the effect upon future sales and the domestic effects of trading or ceasing to trade — for domestic interests will probably include not only the producers and traders, but also groups of people who are hostile towards the adversary for a variety of reasons, and wish to see sanctions enforced.

Such situations do not arise solely within the context of alliances. They may occur as a result of membership of an international organisation, though not often. Economic sanctions were adopted by the League of Nations in 1935 against Italy, and by the UN in 1966 against Rhodesia; in neither instance were they a success. The Rhodesian case is instructive. Sanctions were broken by states with direct interests in the region, like South Africa and Portugal; by states which opposed sanctions as such, especially France; by states mainly concerned with trade including West Germany and Japan; and they were nearly broken by the United States, in pursuance of an abortive congressional move to obtain certain raw materials from Rhodesia. The move was defeated, partly because of opposition from the administration, but also because black votes might be lost through what could be represented as favours to the white government of Rhodesia. It turned out in the end that they were broken by Britain, the very advocate of sanctions, though by multinational oil companies based in Britain rather than through any express decision by the British government. Similar groups of sanction-breaking states will probably emerge from any future proposal for sanctions.

Clearly, there can often be more attraction in the concrete advantages gained by trade, or retained by not forgoing opportunities for trade, than in the warm effects of consolidating an alliance or supporting the concept of collective security. The difference lies in the concreteness. The imposition of sanctions can easily be regarded as merely another diplomatic ploy, embarked upon for reasons of public relations, and designed to impress domestic political supporters and allied states. On the other hand, exports are income. To disturb trade is to disturb the incomes and livelihoods of large numbers of people within one's own country. If it is done, there will probably be demands for compensation for the lost income; even if these are met, a government will have disturbed large numbers of people in respect of matters which are vital to them.

Furthermore, there is a kind of natural separation between trading with a country and approving of the way in which that country's government is carried on. Because governments postulate a total approach to states with which they are in conflict, they are often impelled to argue (and certainly some of their citizens are so impelled) that hostility involves hostility in every respect. Yet this cuts across the interests of trading groups, and, it can often be argued, cuts across the long-term national interest. If the trade in question has been established by reason of comparative advantage, there is every reason to pause before interrupting it. The crisis may pass; attitudes may change on both sides; allies may prove less insistent; income may increase if lines of economic communication are kept open. So far as the allies of the United States are concerned, all these considerations have proved to be correct in respect of restrictions on trade with the Soviet Union and China. They may well be also true of economic relations with Cuba.

This line of thought suggests that the autonomy of the economic world (arising from those inexorable economic 'facts' to which reference has already been made) involves certain 'natural' channels of trade, and certain patterns of economic relationship which are not easily denied, and which reassert themselves if the opportunity arises, but can also be badly disrupted for long periods. West European economic 'integration' (i.e., the influence of persistent patterns of supply and demand, transport and labour supply, within Western Europe) has already been remarked on in Essay 5. The bones of the basic international economy show through, as it were. They can be clothed with political flesh of different kinds, turning them into a variety of figures, but they have a propensity to return to the same sort of image. States are reluctant to disturb this image and these patterns. In consequence, while they may agree with one another at the so-called 'political' level (e.g., about the crises in Iran and Afghanistan in 1980), they may well diverge at the 'economic' level, because of long-term interests which they wish to preserve.

These considerations may not be so important to such massive, multifarious and largely self-sufficient states as the USA and the Soviet Union, each of which can cut off and restore aspects of its trade with little harm to the general state of the economy. They are of much greater importance to the lesser powers mentioned above, to which foreign trade is highly significant and markets are things to retain. Nevertheless, as we shall see in Essay 7, there is no inevitable primacy about 'economic' considerations. States may decide that their alliances are more important than specific economic interests, and that their security will be enhanced by actions which, in the immediate situation, appear to do violence to their economic relations with others; or they may not. There is no obvious rule to apply in such cases, since we are confronted with mixtures of economic interdependence, domestic pressure, alliance obligations and ideological concern, to which each state will respond in its own way.

A related question is whether it is advantageous for states to initiate economic sanctions against others, as distinct from following the lead of a partner in an alliance or the decision of an international organisation. In such cases there is much more freedom of action, since the proposal to initiate economic sanctions can be considered in detail in respect of all the interests involved, before it is made public and attempts are made to enforce it. Rather than being presented to allies as a *fait accompli*, it can be carefully thought out before being applied. The fact that it *can* be thought out is not, of course, any guarantee that it *will* be. It may instead be the sudden decision of politicians grasping at straws, and repenting at leisure when they realise what difficulties they have created for themselves. None the less, a state which initiates proposals of this kind has more chance of making them effective than those which have to join in willy-nilly.

VI

Basically, the economic world is one of livelihoods involving investment, production and consumption, and the political world one of aspirations based upon security, ideology and increasing status. The wish for more worldly goods is a driving force in each. Both involve risks. They intrude upon one another at a great many points. Whatever may be comparative advantage in economic terms can be nullified — perhaps not for long, but certainly for the time being — by political action of a protectionist kind. Whatever may be desired in the way of political advantage may be nullified by sheer lack of resources, and by economic mismanagement emerging in a high level of costs and in balance of payments deficits. The bones of the economic world are always liable to show through, whether it is after a Maoist denial of the significance of international economic facts, a Peronist approach to internal costs, or a Stalinist determination to outrun the development of comparable capitalist states. There is a basic interdependence between states which is inclined to reassert itself; but in any given situation it can be outfaced by political will and by loyalty to the state.

Mentioning political will and the state in this way brings up a question raised in much of the literature about international political economy: whether the multinational corporation is likely to make the state an outworn form of political organisation. Some people have said that its appearance has made the state obsolete. As Robert Gilpin says, the multinational corporation is regarded by proponents of this view

as the embodiment par excellence of the liberal idea of an interdependent world economy. It has taken the integration of national economies beyond trade and money to the internationalisation of production. For the first time in history, production, marketing and investment are being organised on a global scale rather than in terms of isolated national economies. The multinational corporations are increasingly indifferent to national boundaries in making decisions with respect to markets, production, and sources of supply.[11]

Gilpin also points out that, while this development is hailed by some liberal economists as a move towards accelerating the economic growth and welfare of everyone, it is viewed quite differently by 'dependencia' theorists, to whom it represents 'the flow of wealth and benefits from the global, underdeveloped periphery to the centres of industrial financial power and decision'.[12] Where the two schools agree, however, is in allotting an increasing role of influence and independence to the multinational corporation, and a decreasing one to the sovereign state.

Such attitudes have perhaps been shaken in recent years by the experiences of the oil companies, which were archetypal amongst the multinationals, but have had their wings clipped by the oil-producing states. It is true that the companies appear to have made bigger profits, but nobody would suggest that their political influence is as strong as it was before OPEC became a force to reckon with, or that they can do as they wish in non-OPEC countries. Oil is something of a unique industry; others are difficult to compare with it. But the oil example shows that state action can be effective in curbing the power of international business, and in rearranging a whole industry on a global scale. Other multinational corporations have taken notice of the warning which the oil companies represent.

In any case, it is doubtful whether multinational corporations have themselves envisaged a world of diminished sovereign states which they dominated, as some of the more excitable theorists have. For one thing, this domination could credibly apply only to those states in which the multinationals were responsible for the greater, or a vital, part of total economic activity. For another, the multinationals (apart from the mining companies) operate mostly in the rich countries, in which their activity may be prominent but is rarely vital. It would, for example, be bad for the British motor industry if Ford and General Motors pulled out; it would not destroy the British economy or the British state.

Two sorts of multinational have dominated much of the discussion: one which is most common in poor countries and one which matters more in the rich ones. Those in the extractive industries, of which Rio Tinto Zinc would be an example, are the first sort, and the automobile manufacturers, such as General Motors, the second. (A third, the producer and processor of tropical produce, of which Unilever might be regarded as typical, has received rather less attention — perhaps because it has been on the defensive since decolonisation got under way.) The mining companies can decide whether or not to provide the massive investment needed to make idle resources a means of income; if they are not satisfied with the proposals made to them by the state, or with the conditions imposed once the investment has begun, they can leave the minerals in the ground and go somewhere else. The automobile companies can decide whether a country has a motor industry or not — although, as with the mining companies, they have to be unanimous in rejection if the country is to go without. In both instances the state is assumed to have the choice between accepting the multinationals' demands, doing without the industry, or trying to find the capital itself while aware of its own lack of capacity in respect of production and marketing. If it accepts the multinational demands, it must do what it is told, or face the consequences.

It may well be that some states find themselves in just such a situation.

It is doubtful, however, whether many do, and, if they do, whether they are necessarily in a weaker position as states. Many of the ambitious claims about the power of multinationals were made in the confident atmosphere of rapid economic growth in the 1960s and early 1970s, a period in which US official pressure for a liberal world economy was great, investment capital was widely available, demand for raw materials and processed goods was high and rising, and poor countries often felt impelled to accept the propositions of multinationals as an earnest of their belief in economic growth. The more restricted economic climate of the late 1970s and the 1980s makes multinational investment often less attractive to investor and host country alike. In any case, some states have already worked out ways of mitigating the harshness of the state-multinational contest as envisaged by both friends and foes of the multinationals.[13]

States can nationalise the operations of multilateral corporations, with compensation, and can then negotiate with the corporations to run the installations for them, as happened with the copper mines in Zambia. They can extend these service contracts in other directions. They can demand a share in the equity for their own investors, or for the state itself. They can adjust taxation in various ways. They can make deals with rival corporations, especially those based in rival countries. It is also sensible to suggest, as the Brandt Commission does:

> As developing countries acquire more technological skills of their own they should be in a better position, where appropriate, to unpackage the 'technology-invesment package', separating out the components of investment, technology, management and marketing, and importing only what they need and using their domestic inputs wherever they can. There are signs too that corporations are becoming more flexible in negotiating conditions for ownership and concluding licences for pure technology, joint ventures, production-sharing and other looser forms of technology transfers.[14]

If one deliberately chooses 'worst case' examples, any proposition of doom can be demonstrated. It is like this with multinationals. The worst cases — such as those of long standing in Central America — have clearly sapped the independence and integrity of the states in which they occurred; yet the states have survived. A genuinely weak state has never needed multinationals to finish it off. It may suddenly collapse under the pressure of any group with overwhelming arms or money, or more slowly under the effect of years of attrition and corruption from interested parties bent on a different regime.[15] In the contemporary world, as suggested earlier, there are more defences for the weak state against such publicly-defined, high profile dangers as those represented by the multinationals, than for the inexperienced weak states of the nineteenth century.

There is another side to the situation. Those who suggest that multinationals will displace the state or render it redundant usually assume that the state will remain as it was while this process is going on, or will be in a worse condition than ever because of social disruption. Such an argument piles one worst case on another. It would be more realistic to assume that multinational contact could strengthen the state, since multinationals provide an enlarged tax base, thus enabling the state to raise and spend more money. Some of this will go on the services needed to cope with social changes following industrialisation in particular areas. Some of it will go on education provision, because the multinationals need workers with skills and literacy. Multinationals pay their workers more than they got before; this creates groups with a vested interest in further modification of the economy. The effect of multinationals, on the whole, is to make the society richer and more varied and the state more active in its operations. All this is quite consistent with changes in the actual government, as new interests emerge; but this does not mean any necessary diminution in the significance of the state. It may mean quite the reverse.

Experience suggests that, in many instances, the very foreignness of the multinationals enables governments to use them as Aunt Sallys, to be blamed for economic ills, admonished when their promised results do not appear, and held in jeopardy if they are inclined to talk back. It is true that the corporations have the option of diverting their investments elsewhere; but this may often entail serious loss, may affect their reception in other countries, and may open up opportunities for rival firms. In such cases, the whiphand is with the state, so long as state machines are well enough organised to use it. Many, perhaps most, are. Mr Baldwin would find it harder now to set Ishmaelia by the ears. 'Sudden or extreme violence' would be very difficult to exert.

VII

The multinational issue is one, like integration, in which the combined efforts of politicians and scholars can create the appearance of reality when reality is liable to be strikingly different. To deny that multinationals will render the state redundant is not to say that every state will deal successfully with them, or that every state is capable of displaying effective economic policy. There is still scope in the economic world for 'banana republics', though not for all the poor states to become such. Multinationals show that, in certain situations, economic efficiency will provide results which no sovereign state will be prepared to do without, even if it means some concession to what the corporations demand. At the same time, the capacity of states to make life difficult for arrogant corporations operating within their boundaries is now substantial and is being added to, if only in terms of public relations, by the various efforts to provide international codes of conduct for multinationals. It would be an odd firm that failed to take account of this.

The state remains an ambiguous but inescapable factor in the economic world. Its powers of economic control are exercised very much in terms of domestic circumstances, but often with significant effects upon other states. It is to control these effects, in the mass, and to press for changes in the international system, again in the mass, that bodies such as OECD and the IMF exist. They are the political forums within which the rules of the international economic game are put together, through the pressures of differing state interests and some dim awareness of the interests of the whole. In this process, as in the day-to-day mechanics of trade, states continue to be the units that matter most.

Notes

1. Peter B. Kenen and Raymond Lubitz, *International Economics*, 3rd edn (Englewood Cliffs, NJ, 1971), pp. 4-5. It would be good for contemporary economists if they read Friedrich List's *National System of Political Economy* as well as Adam Smith. A useful introduction is Margaret E. Hirst, *Life of Friedrich List and Selections from his Writings* (London, 1909).

2. Two people who deserve praise for their efforts in this direction are Susan Strange and Charles Kindleberger. See Susan Strange, 'International Economic Relations, I: The Need for an Interdisciplinary Approach', in Roger Morgan (ed.), *The Study of International Affairs* (London, 1972), and Charles P. Kindleberger, *Power and Money: The Economics of International Politics and the Politics of International Economics* (New York, 1970). See also C. Fred Bergsten and Lawrence B. Krause (eds.), *World Politics and International Economics* (Washington, 1975).

3. I am aware that Canada has placed heavy restrictions on foreign investment (much more so than Australia); but it would still include suitable investment as amongst its external economic aims, and would form a contrast to the official Third-World line, which treats foreign investors with considerable suspicion.

4. Susan Strange, *International Monetary Relations*, vol. 2 of *International Economic Relations of the Western World* 1959-1971, ed. Andrew Shonfield (London, 1976), pp. 26-7.

5. Evelyn Waugh, *Scoop* (London, 1938), Book 2, ch. 5, p. 1.

6. There are numerous examples of this kind of argument. One which is typical but

may be unfamiliar is Harold J. Laski, 'The Economic Foundations of Peace', in Leonard Woolf (ed.), *The Intelligent Man's Way to Prevent War* (London, 1933), pp. 499-547.

7. For a brisk run through the various schools, and a wide range of references, see Ralph Pettman, *State and Class: A Sociology of International Affairs* (London, 1979), ch. 5.

8. It is not often realised from what slender bases such analyses as Hobson's proceeded. A brief period in South Africa, just before the Boer War broke out, gave Hobson the impetus he needed. (See J.A. Hobson, *Confessions of an Economic Heretic* (London, 1938), ch. V.)

9. Klaus Knorr, *Power and Wealth: The Political Economy of International Power* (London, 1973), p. 78.

10. This name is still used for the group of states which caucus for the achievement of an NIEO, although the number has grown well beyond the original 77.

11. Robert Gilpin, 'Three Models of the Future', in Bergsten and Krause (eds.), *World Politics and International Economics*, pp. 39-40. The whole article is of great interest. It is highly relevant to the matters discussed in this essay.

12. Ibid., p. 43.

13. See Peter P. Gabriel, 'The Multinational Corporation and Economic Development' in Robert E. Hunter and John E. Rielly (eds.), *Development Today* (New York, 1972), pp. 187-91.

14. *North-South: A Programme for Survival,* Report of the Independent Commission on International Development Issues, Chairman, Willy Brandt (London, 1980), pp. 191-2.

15. For the latter process in what was once a sovereign state, see Gavan Daws, *Shoal of Time: A History of the Hawaiian Islands* (Honolulu, 1974), chs. 5-7.

'Interdependence' is a word that, like 'peace', 'freedom' and 'democracy', is used for debating rather than scholarly purposes. It can be made to mean almost any sort of active relationship between states or any other entities; but it usually means '*my* sort of interdependence', just as, in much discussion, 'democracy', 'freedom' or 'peace' means '*my* sort', the sort which suits me and my interests. Dealing with such words presents major problems of definition. One sometimes wonders whether they should be done away with altogether.

There is still, however, some core of meaning left when the hubbub has died down. When states are said to be interdependent, it is because their actions affect one another — although questions of how much they affect each other, whether the effects are symmetrical or asymmetrical, whether the relationship is beneficial to both, and so on, still remain to be settled. In addition, we need not confine ourselves to specific state *actions*; what happens *within* a state may affect what happens in another. Influences arising from changes in taste, technology and the like can affect producers and consumers in a number of states, whether the states involved have official policies in the matter or not. Similarly, the presence of immigrants in country A from country B will create a sense of interdependence whatever attitudes the governments take. Interdependence may be a fact independent of governments, or one created by governments, or both.

Keohane and Nye, with their notion of 'complex interdependence', approach this state of affairs, though the idea as originally stated is largely concerned with official relations between states. However, their notion of 'multiple channels' and their 'economic process model' of interdependence, do help to explain what they call 'international regime change'. In this way, they illuminate the official and unofficial processes constituting the web of connections that most people have in mind when they say that we live in an interdependent world.[1] It is true that if we say this, and say no more, we beg all the interesting questions about how lopsided the interdependence is, what forms it takes and how many countries it involves. These questions need to be tackled in detail. The answers do not affect the fact that in recent times there has been a remarkable increase in the number and nature of transactions between states, not only in goods but also in knowledge and ideas.

This essay is concerned with a particular aspect of the interdependence argument — with the problem of whether economic interdependence creates something of a world society. In this context, economic interdependence is taken to mean a high degree of mutual need arising from trade and investment within the international economy; in effect, the customer is not only assumed to need the banker, but the banker is also assumed to need the customer. There is perhaps something grotesque, even repulsive, in the idea that there is interdependence between the Indian villager and the New York banker, considering the difference in their incomes; yet the fact remains.

The useful categories clearly defined by Alex Inkeles[2] (interconnectedness, autarky, dependence, interdependence, integration, hegemony and convergence) are essential when one is trying to describe the connections between particular states, but will not be used in this essay, because it is concerned with the worldwide condition of economic interconnectedness and interdependence, from which it is assumed that all states draw some benefit. In this context the variations in benefit are less important than the fact that all states participate in international trade, and most in international investment. When one is asking whether particular people constitute a society, one does not require them all to benefit equally before declaring that they belong; it is the fact of persistent relationships between them, rather than their equality or otherwise within these relationships, that decides the answer.

I

Long before contemporary scholars began to investigate economic interdependence in the 1960s, the notion had been widely publicised (indeed, it can be traced back to Adam Smith, and to the enthusiastic support for it by Marx and Engels in the *Communist Manifesto* of 1848). Two studies published in 1914 and 1916 respectively, by Norman Angell and Arthur Greenwood,[3] provide an indication of what economic interdependence looked like before it was treated as a scientific category.

Angell's thesis, a reworking of his argument in *The Great Illusion*, first published in 1909, was that 'co-operation between nations has become essential for the very life of their peoples', and that the need for cooperation had 'rendered the exercise of force by one State against another, for economic, moral or intellectual purposes, futile, because ineffective and irrelevant to the end in view'. Angell saw progress as essentially international: 'We all owe our civilisation to foreigners.' To him, economic interdependence was the symbol and much of the substance of the advantages to be gained. He was concerned to deny what he regarded as 'diplomatic orthodoxy', the view that the survival of a national unit depended upon the physical force which it could exercise against competitors. Angell recognised that competition was a feature of international economic life, but pointed to the vast network of transactions that enabled communities to benefit from economic interchange, and the other vast network of credit which sustained it. The state, in his view, could not through policy provide its citizens with the degree of welfare which international commerce provided; and if the state went to war to achieve what it regarded as its interests, it would emerge the poorer, because 'any State destroying wealth in another must destroy wealth in its own', since international economic activity took place across state boundaries. Angell's main concern was to attack the notion that either extreme economic nationalism or war in pursuit of territory and resources could benefit a people in the long run. Sadly for him, the outbreak of World War I convinced many people that Angell had prophesied that war was impossible, whereas he had said it was quite possible but not at all sensible; he spent the rest of his life rebutting the mistaken interpretation of his work.[4]

The kind of situation which most impressed Angell arose from the international division of labour, and the diffusion of finance capital across boundaries. His position can be gauged from the example in the following quotation:

> Co-operation between nations has become essential for the very life of their peoples. But that co-operation does not take place as between States at all. A trading corporation called 'Britain' does not buy cotton from another corporation called 'America'. A manufacturer in Manchester strikes a bargain with a merchant in Louisiana in order to keep a bargain with a dyer in Germany, and three or a much larger number of parties enter into virtual, or perhaps actual, contract and form a mutually dependent economic community (numbering, it may be, with the work-people in the group of industries involved, some millions of individuals) — an economic entity so far as one can exist which does not include all organised society. The special interests of such a community may become hostile to those of another community

but it will almost certainly not be a 'national' one, but one of a like nature, say a shipping ring or groups of international bankers or Stock Exchange speculators. The frontiers of such communities do not coincide with the areas in which operate the functions of the State . . .

. . . [The] political and economic units do not coincide; and . . . action by political authorities designed to control economic activities which take no account of the limits of political jurisdiction is necessarily irrelevant and ineffective.[5]

Angell was thus primarily concerned with conditions that had grown out of free-trade policies, and were opposed to mercantilist and other restrictive policies. This view of the world, akin to that which Adam Smith bequeathed to the economists of the twentieth century (as suggested in Essay 6), rejected the sovereignty of the state in favour of the Great Commercial Republic composed of the countries which trade with one another. His picture of economic 'communities' bears a close relationship to more recent accounts of the activities of multinational corporations. It is often stated that these bodies are so significant in the economic lives of various countries that they negate the political aims of the governments involved — in other words, they are often (perhaps habitually) greater than states.

Let us now turn to Greenwood, who wrote after World War I began (thus differing from Angell, whose thesis was propounded before the war broke out). Greenwood saw economic interdependence as a consequence of the Industrial Revolution:

The keynote of the change that it has wrought is economic interdependence. The economic self-sufficiency of the Middle Ages has passed away. The countries of Europe not only rely on each other for the satisfaction of many of their needs, but draw their supplies of food, raw materials and manufactured goods from distant parts of the world. In spite of protective tariffs, a rough kind of territorial division of labour has taken place. Far from perfect though it may be, it has nevertheless increased the dependence of nations on each other . . . The enormous growth of foreign trade during the past century is witness of the phenomenon that nations no longer stand alone, and that the world has become — or rather is increasingly becoming — a single economic unit.

Capital, once viscid and sluggish in its flow, has now become liquid, finds little obstacle in political boundaries or natural frontiers, and pours its fertilising stream into the undeveloped regions of the world.

Even labour, notwithstanding the ties of home, of friends, and of familiar institutions, has become much more mobile than early economists would have expected. The concessionaire, the modern Pied Piper of Hamelin, has by the music of higher wages called to him not only white, but also coloured labourers, with far-reaching consequences.

Parallel with the growth of a world-wide economic intercourse — the 'cosmopolitanisation' of industry and commerce — there has been, necessarily, the development of a world system of exchange, of a means of settling debts owed, say, by a British cotton merchant to an American exporter, and of projecting capital and credit, say, from London to the oil-fields of Southern Russia . . .[6]

Greenwood was thus as much aware as Angell of the complex character of economic interdependence. He was also aware of how political unification of the world had lagged behind its economic unification (comparatively speaking), and of how states, through a variety of means such as tariffs, bounties, boycotts and restrictions on the export of capital, pursued their view of national interests by distorting the free flow of resources. Writing after more than a year of experience of the effects of war, he commented, as it were, upon Angell's forebodings:

It had been thought that a great war would work such economic disaster that its end would be a matter of weeks or at the most months. The fact is that the efficiency of production, the technical knowledge, the power of organisation which have assisted in unifying the economic world, and added to the awful thoroughness of war, are instruments in the hands of belligerent states for the purpose of organising for war. The adaptability and resourcefulness of modern industry and commerce, the power to distribute the enormous financial burden over generations, will work to overcome the smashing blow which war gives to society. The very qualities which have developed the world organisation of industry and commerce, and which control it in times of peace, are devoted to adapting it to the different needs and circumstances of war. The growing interdependence and complexity of international economic relations will not render war impossible, but they will make it more and more costly. But even here the extraordinary recuperative powers of the economic organism, the greater knowledge of economic phenomena and, therefore, the greater possibility of control, together with the increased willingness of modern states to institute control, will tend to diminish the net loss of warfare.[7]

What is notable about the extended treatment given to economic inter-dependence by both Angell and Greenwood is the extent to which they divorce economics from politics, so that each has a separate domain, in spite of some overlapping. Both put great stress on nationalism and national prestige as motive forces behind foreign policy, while recognising that foreign offices frequently try to maximise economic advantage by some political move, such as Japan made against China in 1915. They see organised economic interests as influencing government policies in certain directions and up to a certain point. Neither has the sense of ineluctable pressure of economics upon politics that is a feature of J.A. Hobson's *Imperialism* (1902), Lenin's *Imperialism* (1916) and H.N. Brailsford's *The War of Steel and Gold* (1914), all of which, in their different ways, describe capitalist countries as pushed into oppression and hostility by the demands of their capitalists. Angell and Greenwood both see that economic advantage in the widest sense can be reduced by concentration upon national political goals. They see the origins of those nationalist policies, however, much more in notions of military supremacy and apparent national strength, and in the notion of permanent potential hostility between major powers, than in the inevit-able tensions of capitalism. Capitalism, in their view, inclines rather towards internationalism, because capitalists can make most money from a free flow of resources to where they can be put to specialist use.

On the whole, both writers' basic notion of economic interdependence is of a force which will win in the end, in the sense that the advantages which peaceful economic cooperation brings will outweigh those which can be gained from narrowly nationalist policies. Greenwood, however, as the second quotation above shows, recognised that the means developed to serve economic interdependence could also be used to further nationalist ends; and this was one of the reasons why he (and Angell, Hobson and Brailsford) concerned themselves during and after World War I with ideas of containing national power through bodies like the League of Nations, and preventing it from pushing too far into the economic field by internationalising basic resources in some way or other. There is a striking parallel with some contemporary schemes for internationalising the seabed and Antarctica.

II

It was plain to Angell and Greenwood that some sort of society had been created by the process of interdependence which they described. The principal enemy of that society was the rampant sovereign state, under the control of politicians, diplomats and military leaders imbued with the idea that hostility was a natural condition between states and that nothing must stand in the way of the consolidation of national power. Their problem in defining and characterising the kind of world society which they felt vaguely to have come into existence can be expressed in one of Angell's statements: 'the political and economic units do not coincide'. They could not incorporate the sovereign state effectively into what was essentially a free-trade vision. They saw a world which appeared to be unifying itself economically and yet tearing itself apart politically, and in which, moreover, the political units had command of longstanding loyalties, and powerful and significant symbols. They feared the political units as likely to damage the economic units (i.e., to disrupt those chains of economic connection which crossed national frontiers in order to provide tangible benefits in the form of goods and services). They had no substantial form of argument against strong-minded governments, except the well-established free-trade plea that men should recognise that their interests were ultimately not to be served by narrow nationalist policies. Far from seeing economic forces take over governments, they were afraid that governments would become supreme over economic forces to everyone's ultimate disadvantage. Economic interdependence was thus not enough to ensure that world society would develop its own modes of social order and control.

Such attitudes need to be considered afresh at the present time. Talk about interdependence today is often as all-embracing as Angell's conviction that 'war, even when victorious, can no longer achieve those aims for which peoples strive',[8] though the same fear of unilateral state action is not expressed with the same fervour. There is a widespread belief that states are not strong enough to decide their own policies; yet one can also argue that the capacities of states to discipline economic entities such as multinational corporations has increased, and is likely to increase more rapidly than the strength of the corporations themselves.[9] Whether states, in exerting such discipline, are cutting off their noses to spite their faces is another matter. The crucial question is whether they can exercise the sort of power which so disturbed the liberal thinkers of the 1910s; and, on the whole, the answer is that they can.

Economic interdependence is still a fact of great moment, but it has been much affected by political changes since World War I. These include the creation of communist economies in Europe and Asia, the increase in the number of sovereign states following the dissolution of the

European empires, the growth of international regulatory bodies such as GATT and the IMF, and changes in the scope of ecomomic control and provision by sovereign states at large.

The doctrine of mutual benefit through free trade continues to have a place in national policies, as seen in the attempts at mutual lowering of tariffs in GATT, and in the creation of free-trade areas between given states such as those of the EEC. At the same time, trade barriers of various kinds have been accepted as normal instruments of national policy, and the logic of the position held by Angell and Greenwood — that the most important economic units are separate from the political units — has been denied by widespread practice:

> Internal trade is among 'us'. International trade is between 'us' and 'them', as Friedrich List said more than a century ago. Among ourselves, we are prepared to operate a common set of rules, based on a common set of values . . . 'We' adhere to a single monetary, wage, fiscal, commercial policy which affects all individuals within our boundaries regardless of their location. Between 'us' and 'them', our government's task is to take care of us, and theirs to take care of them, using whatever monetary, fiscal, commercial and other national policies may be necessary to do so.[10]

This task, which is specifically the sovereign state's, is the source of the politics of international economics. When states carry out the task described by Kindleberger, they do not deny economic interdependence, but seek to influence it to their own advantage. If we regard the world as a society in which international division of labour has something of the same function as division of labour within a particular national society, then the policies of states are intended to produce a result akin to that which the political efforts of economic interest-groups achieve within the national society, i.e., to affect the interdependence between them so as to benefit workers as against farmers, or businessmen as against workers, or one region against another. To operate in this way is not to destroy the essential interdependence of the domestic economy, but to make it work in a particular way if only for the time being. Similarly, states try to manipulate the system of international economic interdependence so as to suit their interests as seen by governments. Revolutionaries might argue that the interests have been perceived in the wrong way, so as to benefit compradores, multinational corporations and the like; but even if the interests were altered, the procedures would be much the same, although the extent of participation in the international economic system by a given state might change.

In the light of the divisions within the existing interdependence between states, it is appropriate to ask to what extent that interdependence contributes towards the existence of a world society; but first it is necessary to ask what is meant by a society and how it applies to the world.

III

There is a forest of definitions of society; the further one goes into this forest, the less light seems to be thrown on the problem. To say that society is 'the web of social relationships', as MacIver and Page do,[11] is not very helpful. To say that 'each aggregate of human beings of both sexes and all ages bound together into a self-perpetuating group and possessing its own more or less distinctive institutions and culture may be considered a society'[12] is nearer the mark, but it leaves great opportunities for divergent interpretations of what should be included in 'institutions and culture'. Whatever definition is used, one has the problem of how far it should be extended. We can speak of local society, in the sense of the social group in an isolated village or valley, or even in a suburb; we can also speak of national society, as when we say that French society has certain characteristics (which we may, however, have to extend to French-speaking portions of Belgium and Switzerland); and we can extend the sense to areas much wider than a particular country by saying with Simmel that a society is 'a number of individuals connected by interaction'.[13]

It is perhaps unfair to pick out these definitions and put too much weight on them, since each is a shorthand description of something which its author needs a great deal of space to describe fully. I have found it more helpful to take Percy Cohen's discussion of social order,[14] since the question of how much or how little order there is in the international system is obviously of major importance in deciding whether there is a world society or not. Cohen distinguishes five meanings for the term 'social order', all of which, in his view, are both logically and empirically related. They are a certain restraint, especially of violence; some mutuality or reciprocity in social life; some predictability, so that people know what to expect of one another; consistency; and persistence. Each of these meanings represents an aspect of social order; but Cohen makes the point that the opposite of each is also an aspect of social life, which displays violence as well as restraint, opposition as well as reciprocity, uncertainty as well as predictability and consistency and change as well as persistence. If the opposites are uppermost, Cohen seems to be saying, there will be no social order. In fact, however, social order is usually maintained, though sometimes precariously.

Cohen then moves to the various explanations of social order which have been advanced by social theorists. First is that of coercion: men do what they are told by those with the power to tell them. Second is that of interests: men either consciously or unconsciously preserve social order because they find it in their interests to do so. Third, value-consensus: men agree to order because they share certain values, which are predominantly moral but may be also technical and aesthetic. Fourth, inertia: men adhere to social order because that is what they are used to, and a number of mutually reinforcing processes preserve it without direct intention. In each case Cohen elaborates the theory and criticises it. His conclusion is that, while none of the theories can adequately explain the origins of social order, each of them contributes to the explanation of how social order persists, and how it breaks down and changes. Each states a necessary, though not a sufficient, condition for the continuity of any social order. 'All social order', he says, 'rests on a combination of coercion, interest and values'.

I find this a reasonable and illuminating account of what we would look for if we were wanting to say whether a particular aggregation of activities constituted a society. Obviously 'society' is a kind of ideal type, a figurative notion which can be related to so many differently sized and constituted entities or apparent entities that it does not have much use in itself. But a concept of 'social order' which includes the notion of social disorder (i.e., the opposites, or effect of the opposites, of the constituents of social order) is much more realistic and more applicable to the question of whether there is a world society, which in itself is a somewhat figurative use of language.

If we look at economic interdependence in terms of Cohen's five meanings or aspects of social order, it is apparent that elements of each are present in the system of international trade, investment and currency. Restraints are present in the respect for rules of payment, navigation, and the like; there is a network of institutions based upon restraint and reciprocity, and mutuality is recognised in the existence of GATT and the relationships observed between currencies, as well as in the payment of interest and repatriated profits on international investment. There is predictability in forward trading on commodities and in the great network of expectations on which investment and trade are based. There is, as suggested in Essay 6, a considerable element of persistence, which can survive even the excesses of political catastrophe. The system of interdependence is variable, both in the sense that some countries obviously benefit more from it than others, and in the sense that the elements of interdependence do not apply to all countries (investment, for example, does not apply between the capitalist and socialist countries in the same way or to anything like the same extent as between capitalist countries). None the less, it is sufficiently widespread for us to say that Cohen's aspects of social order can all be found.

So, of course, can their opposites: there is an absence of restraint in some countries' approach to their weaker associates' interests; there is uncertainty about future prices and the availability of future investment as well as about the relations between currencies; and the persistence of trade and investment patterns may be disrupted by technical innovation, changes in profitability, or war. The question is whether we judge these opposites to have so much power that they disrupt the idea of social order. I should say that, viewing the world as a whole, there is evidence of *a* social order emerging from economic interdependence. It is lacking in consistency in its impact on different states, but sufficiently evident for us to accept it as a fact. In this sense, we can say that economic interdependence creates a kind of low-level social order for the world as a whole. We can adapt Cohen's explanations, also, to say that it rests upon a combination of coercion, interest and values so far as commercial transactions are concerned.

Here, however, we must reintroduce Angell and Greenwood and their problems with the place of the sovereign state in the world economic order. Angell would have rejected a state-centric view of international relations; indeed, he attacked it in terms even more ferocious than those used by modern opponents of the 'billiard-ball' view of world affairs.[15] To him, the state exerted an antisocial influence in international life, not unlike the influence which Kropotkin ascribed to it in national life: it would, in the interests of an influential few, distort and restrict the opportunities of the many. Yet it was there. As Greenwood saw, it would continue to operate as a powerful, sometimes all-powerful, influence in deciding the way in which peoples would participate in the interdependence of the flow of goods and services within the international system.

Any view of world society, or world social order, must incorporate the sovereign state as an essential actor or element, and must decide how states operate within the world system, in comparison with how they operate within those national systems which are our normal frameworks for considering relations between state and society. Internationally, states operate as large-scale pressure-groups within a total world economy. They have weapons which pressure-groups do not normally have within a peaceful pluralist domestic economy: in the last resort they can back up their demands with threats of force. States provide the aspect of violence, or threatened violence, which is the opposite of Cohen's restraint; but they also provide the aspect of restraint, in the sense that laws made by states enable the systems of payment, navigation, transfer of funds, etc., to be honoured. In most cases, they do not themselves make the contracts, sail the ships or store the goods; but they provide the backing and sanctions which these activities require. In a sense, they constitute both the interests and the authorities for the international economic system, if we wish to nominate parallels with a domestic economic system in which there is only one government.

What states have, in the international economic system, is the power to disrupt and restrict that system. Such a power is only partly paralleled by interest-groups within a domestic pluralist society. It is notable, however, that even when such disruption has taken place through the action of states in a disastrous war, the network of economic inter-dependence begins to re-form itself once the war is over. As suggested in Essay 9, there is often irony in such a process, which makes apparent non-sense of the effort which states have made during the war itself. The strength of the Angell line lies in its awareness, not just of the nonsense, but also of the damage which large-scale wars involve. We should leave open the question whether a more widespread system of economic inter-dependence, made more even-handed by the growth of living standards in the underdeveloped countries, would induce such a sense of social order as would make wars less likely. It seems unlikely, but it is possible.

Two further questions are: What part is played by shared values in the degree of world social order which we can see embodied in economic interdependence? What part is played by international economic order in world order at large?

Cohen says that social order rests on coercion, interests and values. Students of international relations usually have no difficulty in accepting the first and second of these as characteristics of the international system, but are likely to have doubts about the third, if only because the interests of states normally include the preservation and sometimes the extension of the particular sets of institutional values (or ideologies) which they regard as their own.

The problem, as so often, is what one means by values. If security and prosperity are values (rather than goals), then all countries share them. If the interpretation of security and prosperity involves values, then countries differ considerably in the values which they bring to bear, since they differ demonstrably in their interpretations. When they join together in alliances, in order to preserve security, is this a sharing of values? When they join in a customs union, does this involve common values? It seems to me that this kind of activity is much better regarded as a matter of interests, not of values. If, however, one can distinguish between kinds of alliances and customs unions — if, for example, some can be shown to be more a matter of dictation, and others of genuine sharing — then perhaps common values have been at work in the one case and not in the other. I can only conclude that one should be cautious in asserting common values, unless there is clear agreement about what constitutes a value in the particular circumstances being considered. If the search for prosperity involves values, then it is fairly clear that the kind of interdependence discussed in this essay does involve common values to a certain extent, and that these are reflected in the rule-keeping which goes on throughout world trade. In the direct sense, this is a matter of interests; but if interests coincide over a long period of time, as some economic interests evidently do, they may well become shared values, or at least induce harmonious behaviour. It would be most unwise, however, to assume that this behaviour will continue without modification or even contradiction if the pattern of international politics changes.

The second issue is much more consequential. If we agree that a system of social order is discernible in the system of economic interdependence, how are we to see this in the context of world social order, i.e., of a world society at large? Do we say that it constitutes whatever we have, or most of what we have, of world society, and that what is left is not worth talking about? Do we say that there is a greater world society of which this is a lesser though more clearly-defined version? Or do we say that world society is yet to be constructed, and that the low-level version provided by the economic system is a stepping-stone to it?

The further one goes with this kind of enquiry, the harder it is to feel the ground under one's feet. Yet I am satisfied that a concrete system of social order — imperfect, partial and fragmentary though it may be — is embodied in the international economic system. I am also satisfied that states' political behaviour is to some extent (though not inevitably) moderated by their economic interests as reflected in their interdependence with other countries' economies. Yet I do not see a clear causal connection between this situation and what might be called world society at the political level, i.e., at the level of conventional foreign and strategic policy. States can drop their economic involvement overnight if they think the political gains are worth it. This has happened in every war. It was what destroyed the force of Angell's thesis. At the political level, one can see the outlines of another social order, embodying the same names and often connected with the economic one, but independent from it in the sense that the one does not fully fit in its operations with the other. In this sense, though not entirely in Angell's, the economic and political units are not the same. If there is to be a world society in the broad sense, it will exist because of political decision rather than because of economic entanglement; it too will presumably rest upon coercion, interests and values, but probably with the element of coercion as the strongest.

The fact that we can analyse the actions of states as if they were part of a polity consisting of interests and a form of government or authority, in itself suggests that a society must exist in order to give life to that polity. We need not suggest more than a society characterised by frequent outbreaks of anarchy in order to maintain that a sort of social order exists. If the element of coercion increases within the international system — i.e., if 'government', as postulated in Essay 1, becomes a more significant factor — then a world social order will become much more of a self-evident fact than it is at present.

IV

Any view of the influence of economic interdependence in the future must take account of the likely movement of the international economic system, which, like any national system, is subject to fluctuations. For example, it was argued by Gregory Schmid in 1975-6 that:

> (1) we have already reached the end of a 30-year period of growing interdependence; (2) the trend has already reversed itself with national controls rising everywhere; and (3) we are entering, for better or for worse, an era of new mercantilism.[16]

Since this prediction was made, the 'new mercantilism' has increased, causing many Americans to look for increased trade with the uninhibited, rapid-growth economies of East and Southeast Asia, rather than with European countries, where local protectionism appears to be endemic. At the same time, increasing Russian assertiveness in such areas as the Horn of Africa and Afghanistan has, if anything, expanded the importance of NATO countries to American strategy, since, if there were to be eye-ball to eye-ball confrontation between the USA and USSR, the USA would need to be assured of the support of its European allies. The contrast here between the lack of economic opportunities in Europe and the need for military support there emphasises the fact that economic inter-dependence is not the only sort of interdependence. The dependence of states on each other's military and political support may be of more importance, in given situations, than whether their economic gains from trade are increasing or diminishing. Even in times of diminishing economic returns, such as Schmid successfully postulated for the late 1970s and the 1980s, there is likely to be no diminution of military need, provided that a clearly-defined adversary (such as the USSR has been for Western powers for over thirty years) remains in being.

What this means is that 'the overall military structure' plays 'a significant role, under some conditions'.[17] Economic interdependence is not enough. The kind of catastrophe which destroyed Angell's original vision, and which he was so honest and shrewd as to recognise again when it made its approach in the 1930s,[18] is sufficient to overturn the inter-national economic system, not for ever, but for the time being. In these circumstances world social order displays those 'opposites' in Cohen's notion of social order, which are probably indispensable to its operation, but which help to crystallise opposition to the sovereign state as the visible user of violence and as representing 'all the autocratic, arbitrary, coercive, belligerent forces within a social group, a sort of complexus of everything most distasteful to the modern free creative spirit'.[19]

States are easily stigmatised when their participation in world social order appears to be wholly destructive. The difficulty in any effective analysis is to recognise that both destructive and constructive roles are played by states, and that one may be as characteristic as the other. It is foolish to think of only one as being significant, and thereby to neglect or decry the other. The last word may be left to a wise observer of the whole process:

In fact, states can and do co-operate with one another both on a regional and on a global basis. So far is it from being the case that states are antithetical to the need that we recognise to inculcate a greater sense of unity in human society, that it is upon the states-system that our hopes for the latter, at least in the short run, must principally depend. It is the system of states that is at present the only political expression of the unity of mankind, and it is to co-operation among states, in the United Nations and elsewhere, that we have chiefly to look if we are to preserve such sense of common human interests as there may be, to extend it, and to translate it into concrete actions.[20]

Notes

1. Robert O. Keohane and Joseph S. Nye, *Power and Interdependence: World Politics in Transition* (Boston, 1977), chs. 2 and 3.

2. Alex Inkeles, 'The Emerging Social Structure of the World', *World Politics*, July 1975, vol. XXVII, no. 4.

3. Norman Angell, *The Foundations of International Polity* (London, 1914); Arthur Greenwood, 'International Economic Relations', in A.J. Grant *et al.*, *An Introduction to the Study of International Relations* (London, 1916).

4. See his autobiography, *After All* (London, 1951), pp. 143-61.

5. Angell, *The Foundations of International Polity*, pp. xxiii-xxv.

6. Greenwood, 'International Economic Relations', pp. 70-1.

7. Ibid., pp. 99-100.

8. Norman Angell, *The Great Illusion: A Study of the Relations of Military Power to National Advantage* (London, 1912 edn), p. viii.

9. See Richard Haass, 'The Primacy of the State . . . or Revising the Revisionists', *Daedalus*, Fall 1979, pp. 131 ff.

10. Charles P. Kindleberger, 'International Political Theory from Outside', in William T.R. Fox (ed.), *Theoretical Aspects of International Relations* (Notre Dame, 1959), p. 72.

11. R.M. MacIver and Charles H. Page, *Society* (London, 1961) p. 5.

12. Ely Chinoy, 'Society', in Julius Gould and William L. Kolb (eds.), *A Dictionary of the Social Sciences* (London, 1964), p. 674.

13. K. Wolff (ed.), *The Sociology of Georg Simmel* (Glencoe, 1950), p. 10.

14. Percy S. Cohen, *Modern Social Theory* (London, 1968), ch. 2, 'The Central Problems of Sociological Theory'.

15. Angell, *The Foundations of International Polity*, pp. xxvii-xxx.

16. Gregory Schmid, 'Interdependence Has Its Limits', *Foreign Policy*, no. 21, Winter 1975-6, p. 188.

17. Keohane and Nye, *Power and Interdependence*, p. 224.

18. See Angell, *After All*, part III, ch. III.

19. Randolph S. Bourne, 'The State', in *War and the Intellectuals*, ed. Carl Resek (New York, 1964), p. 84. This essay, left unfinished at Bourne's death in 1918, is a powerful polemic against the state.

20. Hedley Bull, 'The State's Positive Role in World Affairs', *Daedalus*, Fall 1979, p. 120.

8 THE RATIONALE OF INTERNATIONAL ORGANISATIONS

International organisations, in particular the 'UN family' composed of the United Nations and its specialised agencies, are unquestionably a part of the international system. Much of the time and energy of foreign offices is taken up with sending delegations to meetings, making sure that qualified people go to specialised conferences, digesting the reports and other paper issued by the organisations and determining what line should be pursued when a particular issue comes up. Conference diplomacy of the UN type bulks larger than at any previous time. In terms of sheer bulk of work, international organisations are a major feature of the international scene.

This has led some people to believe that the growth in bulk is an indication of increasing autonomy for these bodies, i.e., that they are now international actors in their own right and will become increasingly so. It is sometimes suggested that, in tackling worldwide tasks which are beyond the capacity of individual states, they acquire functions and responsibilities which are bound to increase in importance. Some day the organisations may replace the sovereign state in some or much of its present activity, because they have been dealing with matters of global concern, such as the preservation of the environment. The claims made for the future of international organisations vary from person to person; but there is an unmistakable drift, amongst those who have a special interest in them, towards matching global problems with global responsibility.

This essay attempts to examine this notion against the background of the actual performance of international organisations.

I

A number of urges can be seen at work in international bodies. These urges are not all compatible, but they contribute to the kinds of activities that go on. They include, amongst others:

133

— the desire for global cooperation, vaguely present in all countries, and vaguely expressed by states on almost every international occasion. This provides the basic assumption that whatever the UN family is doing must, in a broad sense, be a good thing, though there will be objections from individual states when what they regard as their interests are affected.

— the desire for peace and security, an ever present wish in all countries, but no longer widely regarded as likely to be satisfied by the UN and subsisting mainly as an occasionally expressed need which might one day be filled by a different sort of body.

— the desire for specific cooperation in technical fields such as the eradication of infectious diseases, and the allocation of radio frequencies. The oldest and most stable international organisations are those which meet this sort of need.

— the desire for a forum in which particular states and groups of states can express their wishes and gather support for international action. This aspect of the UN system has grown spectacularly in the past decade or so.

Each of these desires may possess states from regions and groupings throughout the world. They are, in a sense, shared international aims which permit a great variety of interpretations, depending on the specific interests which each state seeks to advance. There are other desires, exhibited in the operation of international bodies, which are less universal, as formulated here, but may occur to any state. They include:

— the desire for recognition, especially characteristic of quite new states which need to display their recently gained sovereignty. It may also be urgent for countries which have lost sovereign status or been denied it by a significant number of existing states. The cases of Ethiopia at the League of Nations, after its defeat by Italy, and more recently of China, Taiwan, the two Koreas and the two Germanies, come readily to mind.

— the desire for superiority (another form of the desire for recognition) over former enemies and over claimants to one's own territory. The activities of both Koreas in seeking UN approval are an example.

— the desire for diplomatic opportunity, which may range in importance from the attempts of small, new states to use UN meetings for contacts which might otherwise require expensive diplomatic missions, to the efforts of states to form coalitions such as the Group of 77. The purpose is to use the machinery of the UN system to advance the joint interests which members of the group agree to express.

Each of these provides some reason for the continuance of the UN system, which gains strength from the fact that a great many states support it in order to satisfy differing desires. Some are common to all however they may be defined in practice; others are more specific and constitute special reasons for support of the system. What is most notable, however, is that each of the desires listed is essentially the aim of a state or states. It may be shared by the peoples involved, but is expressed and interpreted by states. None of them can be represented as an insistent demand that mankind be treated as a whole. The best efforts of idealistic world-government associations have so far failed to produce any such pressures for the transformation and extension of the UN system. Instead, there have been pressures from states to extract, from the system, resources, declarations and facilities which will meet their needs.

The desires listed are, in fact, a series of expressions of national interest. They may descend to the simple wish to stay in the organisation and not be pushed out of it (as with South Africa and Israel) in spite of condemnation of the organisation as a whole; and may ascend to cloudy projects for an extension of UN authority to police schemes for automatic transfer of resources from rich countries to poor. What is abundantly clear, however, is that these aims are formulated and expressed by states, with their own and their friends' interests very much to the fore.

II

Although the preceding paragraph stresses the actions of particular states, it should also be emphasised that states form groups and coalitions in order to gain greater influence over the activities of international bodies. Group organisation is now formally recognised in the operations of the UN. It has become much more systematised than in the early days of the body, when such groups were postulated for the purpose of elections to the Security Council. It also applies in other international bodies where groups, regions and zones are the recognised divisions.

Each coalition or constellation of states which gains control of the majority of votes in the General Assembly claims that its resolutions represent the conscience of mankind. This was certainly the attitude of the coalition led by the United States in the 1950s, as it is of the Third-World coalition which now commands a majority. Under such circumstances the conscience of mankind is automatically adjusted to, say, the needs of the United States in 1956 and the Arabs in 1980. This will be the case with key resolutions on the issues of the moment, and even more so in any extension of UN activities.

Such extension may take several forms. One is to find new functions for existing bodies, often in practice duplicating what is already done by others. Another closely related to it, is to find new interpretations of the Charter, so that there may be an expansion of existing jurisdiction to take in new responsibilities. Most of the specialised agencies have changed the main thrust of their activities since new ex-colonial states began to pour into the system in 1960. Such bodies as ILO, FAO and UNESCO have acquired new preoccupations and devised new services to the under-developed countries. Even the IMF and the World Bank, in which voting goes by economic strength and not by numbers, have revised their functions so as to assist more directly with poor countries' balance of payments problems, and to provide soft loans for development.

A further form in which the extension of UN activities may occur, in partial satisfaction of the wishes of the coalition constituting the majority of the time, is the creation of new specialised UN bodies. An example is the creation of a substantial secretariat for UNCTAD. In the same vein, the UN has seen in recent years the creation of a number of bodies connected with development and designed to advance the cause of the NIEO. With heavy Third-World influence upon the composition of the UN secretariat, the possible staffs of proposed bodies are participants in the business of drawing up their constitutions.

An example of what happens in attempts to set up a new UN agency occurred in August 1979, when a United Nations Conference on Science and Technology for Development (UNCSTD) was held in Vienna. The new body which the conference agreed to set up was promised only a quarter or an eighth of the resources which the organisers hoped for according to the UN's publication *Development Forum* (vol. VII, no. 6, Aug.-Sept. 1979). There had been expectations that it would become responsible for the code of conduct for the transfer of technologies, and for the code on multinational corporations; but the internal politics of the UN system left the first of these with UNCTAD in Geneva, and the second with the UN in New York. There was, however, a minor triumph in relation to ECOSOC, the UN's Economic and Social Council. Before the conference the UN's activities in the sphere of science and technology for development were carried out by a committee under ECOSOC which could amend or suppress its reports. The new body would report through ECOSOC but not to it; the General Assembly would get its reports unchanged. The secretariat of the new body would also have some power over 'coordination' of related activities by the specialised agencies, though not those of UNCTAD. To achieve the results and to capitalise upon them, it was agreed to create a policy-making body which all UN members could join, a secretariat, and an executive agency.

The process of turning old institutions into instruments of particular majority causes, and creating new ones for the same purpose, involves using the machinery of international organisations to serve particular interests. Within the framework outlined in Essay 1, the interests which are dominant for the time being have, in effect, the opportunity of appointing the authorities who will, up to a point, decide the disposition of scarce resources. These authorities (i.e., the new and refurbished international bodies) are not, however, the only ones. The rich countries of the West constitute another set of authorities, self-appointed, whose authority derives from their wealth, and who can reject the transfer of these resources if they so decide. They are largely judges in their own cause, but so are UNCTAD and the other bodies appointed through Third-World influence.

Together, these two sets of authorities — essentially state-centred in the sense that one group of states takes one standpoint and the other takes the opposite — make up the reality of much of what goes on in international organisations. There are times when the second set of interests/authorities may be goaded into taking actions against the first, as when the United States resigned from the ILO, and took its substantial contribution with it. The 'conscience of mankind' thus becomes a highly variable quantity, depending on voting numbers and the level of tolerance of the rich Western countries.

III

International organisations in practice are very much the sum of their parts. They have some, but not much, identity in their own right; in general, they are there to do what a majority of their members wants. The fact that they have staffs of their own, and that these staffs can develop some sense of *esprit de corps* and of a consistent overall policy, means that there are factors working in favour of their developing a certain autonomy; but there are other factors working in the opposite direction.

One of these is the tendency of active, influential members to demand that their own nationals be effectively represented in the secretariats. Salvador de Madariaga has described how the secretariat of the League of Nations was nullified by the appointment of politically inspired staff, on which the Italian, German and other governments insisted. He believed that it was prevented from being 'a centre of calm and common sense in the entangled net of international tensions'.[1] In recent times, much the same effect has resulted, on a larger scale, from the wholesale appointment of Arabs and Africans to international secretariats. Under these circumstances the possibility of the organisation's developing its own persistent policy is diminished, unless it has been created in the first place to satisfy the interests of those states which are pushing for the appointment of their own people.

Another difficulty arises from the awareness of those at the head of international bodies that the balance of numbers amongst the members may shift, and that they must keep their options open for what may be, in effect, a change of government. In their different situations, this problem troubled such secretaries-general as Sir Eric Drummond and Trygve Lie, and, in contrast, provided new opportunities for Dag Hammarskjold. There was no question of avoiding a change of regime. The problem was one of timing, of when the change would take place; and Hammarskjold was fortunate in that it occurred just when he needed it. Few secretaries-general have been so fortunate as Albert Thomas, who was able to create the ILO almost single-handed and decide what form it would take and which course it would follow.

The difficulty of establishing and developing traditions in international bodies, in the face of pressures from interested groups of states, is a reason for thinking that the theories of functionalism will not work in this sphere any more than in the context of regional integration, which was considered in Essay 5. David Mitrany's pamphlet, *A Working Peace System*, which started this particular hare in 1943, envisaged a situation in which functional international bodies, not unlike the specialised agencies, would increasingly assume responsibility for economic management, and would, by their success, induce a spirit of international cooperation. They would eschew politics and concentrate on economics. He relied heavily on detached, objective views of general welfare, expressed and implemented by international civil servants. The present circumstances are very different. They, like most other circumstances of international bodies, suggest a dominance by sovereign states which Mitrany would have found repugnant to his ideas.[2]

IV

In this connection, perhaps Mitrany was wrong to distinguish so sharply between politics and economics. By politics he meant the arguments over peace and war, boundaries and minorities, which had bedevilled Europe before and during two world wars. His hope was that the nationalistic passions aroused by these issues, which were highly explosive and led easily to war, would not appear in respect of the more humdrum issues of economics. His thinking was rather in the Cobdenite tradition. Cobden's motto of 'no foreign politics!', and his emphasis on the improvements in international understanding likely to result from increased trade, have much in common with Mitrany's distinction.

A basic difficulty is that international trade, currency and investment are humdrum only so long as they take place either between equals (the Cobdenite situation), or between a dominant power and other states or colonies which have no chance of objecting to the terms on which the exchanges are conducted (essentially the mercantilist situation). Mitrany's original conception was largely Eurocentric, with special provisions for the European powers' dependencies. As a theory, it now has to face the changed circumstances of a vastly increased number of sovereign states, the majority of which regard economic issues as matters of acute controversy because of the inequalities of the international economy, and are in a position to push their claims in individual terms and as pressure-groups.

Under such circumstances, there is not much likelihood of international economic questions being handled either cooperatively or by detached groups of specialists. In Mitrany's terms, economics becomes politicised, and begins to exhibit many of the adversary characteristics which troubled him about questions of boundaries and minorities. Any international organisation created to deal with the situation will hardly be humdrum in operation, unless it proves a failure at securing any automatic transfer of resources, and retreats to the customary task of shifting paper about.

Much vague talk of interdependence in the context of international organisations has assumed that the dichotomy between the sovereign state on the one hand and the international body on the other is the important one. If a task such as the development of Antarctica or the pollution of the atmosphere or the improvement of the poorest countries' lot is to be undertaken, it will prove too large for individual states. Accordingly, it must be done by international bodies — which, by implication, are unitary in character and capable of sound global judgements. In fact, while the dichotomy is formally correct, it neglects the manifestly non-unitary character of international bodies. As a matter of practical politics, coalitions such as the Group of 77 need to be inserted as a kind of middle term between sovereign states and international organisations, since it is they who process the notion of globalism to suit their own interests. They do this through their numbers in the General Assembly and the comparable bodies in the specialised agencies, and through their preponderance in the secretariats.

It is not sufficient to think of international organisations as 'networks of interdependence'[3] which will tackle the global problems about which mankind will become increasingly aware and which provide common interests. The problems posed as global are either capable of being seen in concrete terms of particular states' interests (which is how states will attempt to treat them), or are so inchoate as not to be susceptible to political action. If Plato's philosopher-kings were running the UN, and were accepted as such by the philosopher-kings running individual states, no political problem would arise; the dichotomy of responsibility would be accepted, and all that remained would be the administration of the matters in question. Policy would proceed, not from the clash of state interests, but from general principles. This is not how the system works now. It is inconceivable that the Arab and African states (to go no further) would allow it to work in this way — unless they appointed the UN philosopher-kings, in which case the rich countries might well withdraw from the whole operation.

The reality behind this situation is not simply that states have divergent interests. It is also that 'global interests' are hard to define in any terms which will satisfy all the sovereign states concerned. No matter how a global interest is described, its satisfaction will require that some states gain more than others, and some actually lose. (An example would be the notion that Antarctica should become 'global property'.) If, as is usually the case, it is put in the vaguest terms, and no attempt is made to itemise the costs, it can be made to look as if nobody loses. The representatives of states may accept this in the abstract; they are accustomed to supporting large general propositions, but also to ensuring that the wording is sufficienctly ambiguous to allow them a way out. Once the costs begin to appear, a much more cautious attitude is likely.

The typical reaction of the rich states, in circumstances which appear to demand heavy and continuous levies from them, is to limit both the extent of their contributions and the period in which these will be required. Similarly, poor states, which may be called upon by the proposal to assume commitments which appear to limit their freedom of action, are likely to raise objections and demand more for themselves. They will also be suspicious of any suggestion that rich states should have a say in how their money is spent.

In general terms, international organisations operate so that the states come first and the organisation second. The organisation (i.e., its staff, consultants, etc.) is rewarded for its secondary role by being allowed to present initiatives in implementation of general policies approved by the majority of members, and by the prerequisites of office. In organisations with highly technical tasks, such as coordination of the postal and meteorological systems, much latitude is allowed to the staffs, who share a common technical language with their counterparts in each national government. However, in the bodies concerned with issues of international hostility and with those of transfer of resources, there is much less autonomy. Staffs are cautious in their capacity as international men, often blatant in their furtherance of the interests of their own countries.

The latter development, especially noticeable in regard to the Arab states, has turned most international secretariats into annexes of the Third-World movement. In some ways this is to be applauded. The new states often lack the money and skills to provide themselves with effective diplomatic services; help from UN officials in preparing their briefs is often welcome. The arguments about trade and development are often abstruse, requiring considerable background which the representatives of new states may not possess; it is only fair that they should have expert advice when they need it. There is also the brute fact that the Third-World states are in a majority, and have a right to be heard and listened to in any international context.

However, there is another side to the coin. International organisations may gain in esteem from the services they provide to poor countries, but they may lose through the loss of support from the West on account of their concentration on Third-World issues. The question is complex; it can be persuasively argued that the interests of Western countries are served by concessions to the Third World, and that the UN system, while troublesome when questions arise about Israel and South Africa, is the best general forum in which demands and responses can be made. The future of the system will depend very largely on the decisions of the two sides about how to operate it. But on either side these will be decisions made by states and not by the organisations themselves.

It is a significant aspect of the situation regarding international bodies that one can speak of 'the two sides', as in the previous paragraph, when in fact there is a third side, comprising the Soviet Union and the states which respond to its direction, and a conceivable fourth side, that which might be mobilised by China. However, the two-side formulation corresponds with the actual working of international organisations. Since most of the time of the UN system is taken up with questions of development in one form and another, and since the Third-World states have decided that practically nothing is to be gained from the Soviet Union through the UN, the effective debate is between the Group of 77 and the developed countries of the West, with which they already have extensive economic contacts, and which can be represented, because of colonialism and capitalism, as the source of their ills. The Soviet Union is a spectator at the debate, sometimes displeased when Marxist rhetoric is deserted by the Group of 77 in favour of pragmatic demands within the confines of the free market system, but generally glad that the West should be the target of attack. The watching brief which the Soviet Union holds is likely to become active participation if ever its interests appear to be threatened. There is certainly no wish on the Soviet side to become the object of autonomous action by an international organisation. The same is true of China, and indeed of every member-state, whichever 'side' it is on.

Notes

1. Salvador de Madariaga, *Morning Without Noon: Memoirs* (Westmead, 1974), p. 278.
2. David Mitrany, *The Functional Theory of Politics* (London, 1975).
3. Harold K. Jacobson, *Networks of Interdependence* (New York, 1979), is an impressive recent textbook on international organisations. It includes much discussion of how such bodies may meet future 'global needs'.

9 THE MULTIPLE IRONIES OF THE INTERNATIONAL SYSTEM

The international system is full of bitter, maddening and sometimes comic ironies, which pile themselves one on top of the other to create multiple combinations of ironic amusement, exasperation and regret. This does not mean that the whole system is constantly to be viewed with an eye to irony; but the ironic is never far away, and, if one is not prepared for it, one may be reduced to tears by its continual reappearance.

In this essay various ironic situations are described, and an attempt is made to suggest why they occur so frequently.

I

One of the most striking is the way in which ex-enemies are embraced so soon after the end of a war. This is not a feature of all wars; in recent times it did not occur after the Korean and Vietnam conflicts, although it did happen after the confrontation between Indonesia and Malaysia. The Franco-Prussian war was not noted for it, though the Crimean war was. In the twentieth century the Boer war was an early example. The prime cases, however, have been the two world wars.

Those who lived through World War II will be accustomed to meeting simple, ageing people who are surprised at how quickly the dastardly Germans and Japanese (and, from the other side, the dastardly British, French and Americans) became friends, allies and nice people. Indeed, it is difficult at times for even the most sophisticated to avoid the feeling that something has gone wrong with the system. It seems absurd that five or six years of wholesale destruction should be needed to achieve a result which, on the present showing of former enemies, could have been achieved by negotiation and one or two well-timed assassinations. These feelings must have been even more overwhelming in the 1920s, as the spate of anti-war novels suggests. Such thoughts would have been treason during the wars themselves; whenever they appeared they were hunted down and silenced. They were, of course, rarely expressed by people other than those whose interests harmonised with the other side's. It may still give some of us a warm glow to think that they were never expressed in our hearing. Yet there is a sense in which the war cemeteries and the rebuilt cities of Europe and Asia mock both the protestations of the combatants, and the cosy relationships which exist between them now.

The irony is not, of course, complete. Certain kinds of animosity did survive World War II; some are still current. Until the 1970s, the Chinese government found it convenient to devote films, plays and operas to denunciation of the Japanese just as the Soviet Union and its client regimes in Eastern Europe continue to imply, and at moments of crisis to state, that Nazism is still to be found in West Germany. The Soviet and Japanese governments both find it useful to maximise the importance of Russian retention of the Kurile Islands; each of them hopes that the issue will produce concessions from the other. But these instances suggest at least a degree of contrivance. Whether the same is true of the continued hostility between the two halves of Korea, with its occasional bursts of apparent eagerness for reunion, is very much a moot point. What does seem to be clear is that those dead who fought to exterminate a tyranny embodied not only in a state, but also in a people, can be viewed as having died in vain. This is where irony becomes tragedy. There is, unquestionably, a difference between the present German and Japanese regimes, and those which existed in 1939; but is the difference great enough, and so obviously achievable only by war, to justify the slaughter?

Wars, it seems, produce unintended results which can hardly have been envisaged by those who launched them. Whether the Germans, Austrians, Russians, French or British can be held responsible for starting World War I, none of them can have wanted the Bolshevik Revolution, which was a direct result of the war. Similarly, none of them can have intended the establishment of the state of Israel, which was another result, though longer delayed. If Hitler had known that his invasion of the Soviet Union would lead to communist regimes in Eastern Europe and in half of Germany, he might have hesitated; however, given his maniac disposition, one cannot be sure.

The irony of relationships after a war is directly attributable to the realities of the postwar international system. Once the dust of battle settles, it becomes clear that the atomosphere of a crusade no longer applies, and that potential allies must not be lost on account of their being recent enemies. After both world wars, the decisive influence upon the system was that of the Soviet Union. After World War I, the Western allies were affected by the fear that communist revolution would spread from Russia across Europe, and take particular hold in Germany. After

World War II, they were similarly affected by the fear that Soviet power (i.e., communism now embodied in a heavily armed nationalistic state) would do to the western half of Germany what it was doing to the eastern half which it occupied. Similarly, Japan was viewed, no longer as the aggressor of 1941, but as a prize which the Soviet Union (and later communist China) might covet.

In both cases there was a contrast with the situation after the Franco-Prussian war. Bismarck had nothing to gain, and something to lose, from making friends with France; his aim was to consolidate a strong Germany on the basis of Prussian ascendancy, the reality of which could be demonstrated most effectively by continuing to be severe on France at a time when no other power in Europe was both hostile to Prussia and capable of allying itself with France.

On the other hand, there is a slight similarity between the treatment of ex-enemies by the Western allies after the two world wars, and Britain's treatment of the Boers after the war against them had ended. In this case the defeated Boers had a possible friend in Imperial Germany, which had publicly shown sympathy towards them and was in possession of South-west Africa. There were other reasons for clemency, including the position of the English-speaking South Africans; but the reality of the German presence, at a time when the British government was becoming increasingly aware of German ambitions in Europe, was an influence in its own right.

The other wars mentioned above are all susceptible to the same sort of postwar analysis as that which has been suggested for the two world wars, and the Franco-Prussian and Boer wars; the international system makes its own demands, and interests are rapidly adjusted as new forces and strengths appear. There is, however, a further reason for niceness towards ex-enemies, which has become more important with the growth of the international economy: the difficulty which states encounter if they continue to treat economic intercourse as if it were trading with the enemy.

As we saw in Essay 6, there are certain channels of trade and transport which become ingrained, as it were, and which reassert their significance in spite of political animosities. Whether it is Rotterdam's significance at the mouth of the Rhine, or Japan's interest in Manchuria and Korea, or Zambia's dependence on facilities from Rhodesia (Zimbabwe), there are forces arising from geography and past connection which indicate that the best and safest course is to restore trade as quickly as possible, whether it squares with political rhetoric or not. The world cannot be made to stand still. If in 1980 China finds it profitable to manufacture samurai swords for sale to Japanese tourists and businessmen, the irony must give place to the need for foreign exchange.

The same may be true of potential, rather than past, enemies. In the 1950s and 60s the Australian government felt impelled, because of its close ties with the United States, to withhold formal recognition from the communist government of China, and to join in denunciation of China as a danger to peace. It found, however, that there was a substantial demand from China for wheat, one of Australia's staple exports; and the combination of economic interests with the fear that others might capture the market caused the Australian government to conclude agreements with the Chinese authorities while still refusing to recognise their sovereignty. Similarly, while the government of West Germany refused to recognise that of East Germany, it was shrewd enough to induce the EEC to allow East German goods access to the European Community.

As we have seen, there is something basic about livelihoods; when they appear to be involved, ideology may be discarded. The Soviet Union has made a variety of mutually satisfactory trade arrangements with countries which rhetoric would have suggested were its bitter foes; France and Japan were prominent in enabling the white Rhodesian regime to remain in being in spite of their protestations of support for black African denunciations of it. 'Heart on the left, wallet on the right' is a saying which can not only be applied to states, but also reversed and still remain true. There is a powerful sense in which economic interests override political protestations as we saw in respect of proposals for economic sanctions. Why it is so is not hard to determine; yet there is irony in the eagerness with which governments rush to trade with those states which they have told (and sometimes continue to tell) their people are accursed.

II

Such situations would not appear so ironic if the rhetoric of war had been more restrained. In the 1960s and 70s, it has become the custom in the Western world to ignore or deprecate the crudeness of propaganda normally used in Western societies during wars, and still common form in the Soviet Union, China and the Arab countries where adversaries are concerned. Perhaps the disasters of the Vietnam war have something to do with this sort of emotional withdrawal from past practice; perhaps the preoccupation of strategists with imaginary instant wars with nuclear weapons renders war propaganda superfluous. But a temporary lapse into detached virtue does not mean that virtue will always be present.

War propaganda has normally accused the enemy of both cruelty and racism in its emphasis upon the enemy's atrocious treatment of occupied countries and of other defenceless groups of people such as the European Jews in World War II. However, those who make this kind of accusation can have it levelled against themselves, since usually it is aimed not solely at the governments of the enemy states but at their peoples (if only by implication) and since it is used to justify comparably cruel treatment of the enemy, such as the bombing of Dresden and Hiroshima.

War propaganda is especially ironic when it is the mirror-image of the enemy's. Such an image may involve more than the performance of acts which are the same as the other side commits. It may also involve the use of the same holy books and symbols. The practice of Christian states in World War I, of using the scriptures and the forms of religion to damn their opponents who were doing the same, has been paralleled in recent years by communist states, which use Marx and Lenin to refute one another's policies. Holy books can be used to prove almost anything, if one has sufficient time to search them thoroughly; but there is something grotesque and unseemly about their indiscriminate use, especially if it is in order to justify somersaults from previous positions. There is a crudeness about this sort of theologising, yet it is thought to be necessary. When there are no such books to appeal to, or when they have lost their significance for the people at large (as now seems to be the case in Western countries, and may be occurring in those with communist regimes), the tendency is to substitute such magic words as 'democracy', 'liberation', 'peace', and 'freedom'. As George Orwell made clear in *1984*, these words are just as readily converted to any state's use as the former theologies. The words are not meaningless, any more than the scriptures; but they are so ambiguous that they can be plausibly made to support almost any political interest, however much its practice diverges from the basic meaning of the words.

Another particular aspect of war propaganda — one which is to be found before and after hostilities as well as while they are going on — is the common assertion of both sides that they are engaged in defence rather than offence, and that their weapons follow suit. *We* are defending ourselves; *they* are planning to attack us, or someone else important to us. Sometimes, of course, it is true. But the irony is that, while our defence is said to be deterring them, it is also stimulating them to fresh ingenuity in devising counters to our weapons. Since the purely defensive weapon is a rarity, it is very difficult to distinguish between one preparation for war and another. Both may lead states to the brink, and impel them to take the initiative in jumping over. In the case of such awesome weapons as those with nuclear warheads, it can be argued that rivalry between super-powers leads to a mutually deterrent situation; but if the rivalry turns to constructing 'battlefield' nuclear weapons, those of a minor character which can allegedly be used under controlled conditions, the advantages of deterrence can soon become lost. One is seemingly back with a contest between fieldguns or bombing planes, each side being concerned to maintain to its people and to the world at large that its aims are purely defensive.

One may ask why these ironies are not apparent to the peoples engaged in wars — or, if they are, why more is not said about them. Partly this is because governments discourage such talk, but the main reason is that peoples themselves become impatient with carping criticism when there is a war to win.

A further consequence of the Vietnam war has been that many people in the West, especially the young, are inclined to see all wars in its image, i.e., as the sort of war in which people argue fiercely about whether their government is right to engage in the war, or to support those which do. In this sense the Vietnam war was highly untypical. The United States, in which most argument took place, had not had this experience in the earlier wars in which it had engaged; and the same was true of Australia and Britain.[1] The more typical situation is that of a populace either enthusiastic about the war, or stoically convinced that it is a terrible necessity. Under these circumstances, the deaths in battle of one's own soldiers are the price one pays for a righteous cause; the deaths of the enemy are the prizes gained from undeserving sinners. The proposition will vary from war to war, with least widespread assurance, perhaps, in colonial wars such as those which the British fought against the Boers and the French in Vietnam and Algeria; but it is usually maintained by the majority.

A special case involving war is that of the concept of aggression. For many years after World War II there was a widespread view in the West, and in some of the countries under Western influence, that aggression should be identified in order to prevent a war from breaking out. In the United Nations Charter and elsewhere, the assumption was implicit that wars began with a recognisable act of aggression by one state upon a second state's territory, and that, once identification took place, it would be relatively easy to summon other states to participate in measures of collective security. These would prevent the war from happening, or stop it soon after it began.

This view relied heavily upon the examples of Hitler's successive moves in the 1930s and Japan's attack on Pearl Harbour. It involved the understandable though inexcusable notion that future wars would start in similar ways; it was assumed that Hitler could have been 'stopped' if his earliest act of aggression had been identified as a matter of joint international concern. 'Peace is indivisible' (Litvinov's maxim of the 1930s) became by implication the watchword of those who proclaimed the virtues of collective security, which would manifest itself if only the aggressor could be shown up.

The irony of this interpretation of events arose because it oversimplified the causes of war and provided little or no clue to the problems which the Western powers would in practice encounter in the late 1940s and thereafter. It was essentially a generalisation from one or two cases. It took no account of those complex situations in which states push and pull each other into successive demand and response, with war as the likely outcome. Also, it neglected the possibility that hostile acts, short of war, might create circumstances approximating those of a warlike act. And it gave no credence to the possibility that one's own side might wish to commit ostensibly aggressive acts in order to achieve what it regarded as appropriate and proper ends. In other words, it ignored much of the reality of international politics.

The result has been that, since the 1940s, Western powers have had to approximate aggression as originally defined with whatever the Soviet Union has been doing at the time, whether it was reasserting control over the satellites of Eastern Europe, or encouraging subversion elsewhere. In the same period they have had to excuse simple acts of aggression by themselves and their associates, whether these were CIA activities against Mossadegh in Iran and interference in Guatemala, or the Anglo-French attack on Egypt over the Suez Canal, or the Chinese determination to teach the Vietnamese 'a lesson'. The original assumptions proved to be applicable to the Soviet Union in Hungary and Czechoslovakia, but inoperable in these cases and in that of Afghanistan in 1980; at the same time, they could all too readily be applied to Western actions such as those mentioned above. Because of this irony, and because of a growing Western awareness that the history of World War II was unlikely to repeat itself, 'aggression' ceased to be a watchword and became something of an embarrassment. More complex formulations were needed; yet aggression remained in the international dictionary, even though it had become customary to distinguish between those acts of aggression which benefited one's own side and those which did not. Peace, never truly indivisible, had become decidedly less so.

III

There is a special sort of irony about the way in which the superpowers see themselves in the current international system. Great powers have always taken themselves seriously, expressed vague notions of destiny, responsibility and obligation, and been inclined to dismiss lesser powers as troublesome or insignificant; but there is a special sort of pomposity likely to afflict the leaders of the United States and the Soviet Union. It comes from the uncomfortable knowledge that nuclear weapons may cause enormous destruction if placed in 'the wrong hands', as it is sometimes put. This leads to a conviction that other states should not have these weapons, the assumption being that only the superpowers can be trusted to have them and decide their use. Yet the superpowers spare no opportunity to accuse each other of the worst kind of international behaviour, with the clear indication on each side that the other is not to be trusted. If states below superpower status cannot be trusted with nuclear weapons, even when commended by one of the superpowers on other grounds, why should it be assumed that the superpowers themselves can be trusted, especially when they continue to abuse one another?

The answer, presumably, is that the notion of 'trust' is really inappropriate to the situation, which is essentially one of naked power, of mutual suspicion, of fear that the other superpower may control or influence any new state which acquires nuclear weapons, and of concern that nuclear blackmail may be exercised by any 'rogue' state (i.e., one which will not obey orders or succumb to influence) which may acquire them. Trust is an alien concept in such circumstances. Its use in rhetoric gives a certain gloss to the situation, but lays the superpowers (i.e., the USA rather than the Soviet Union, which does not put much gloss on anything) open to the charge that they are moralising about something which is really beyond morality.

Superpower status entails the delusion that one's own state knows what is best for its allies, and that they are ungrateful if they do not behave as requested. The Soviet Union's relations with Yugoslavia and the United States's with France are examples; perhaps history will show a similar record in relations between China and Vietnam. The irony resides in the simultaneous assertions that members of alliances, or states in some kind of association with one another, are in a condition of sovereign equality, and that the lesser ones should do what they are told. There was a strain of moral outrage in the complaints of the major power in each of the cases cited, notably in unofficial but representative American statements about France when de Gaulle was President.

Moral outrage, hurt pride and puzzlement competed with one another to express the disappointment aroused by France's determination not only to pursue its nuclear programme, but also to refuse to accommodate NATO. Reference has already been made in Essay 5 to American ignorance of the sources of French international behaviour; when to this ignorance is joined resentment at unwarranted independence, one gets an ironic situation in which American claims that France is irrational and effete become increasingly unreal. It is true that the French are often grasping and self-centred, and often drive a hard bargain in their international dealings; but the United States should be used to this by now, and might be expected to show more wisdom and realism in coping with French behaviour. From a French standpoint, which is the only one the French accept, there is always good reason for the line which their country takes. Moreover, France is central to any notion of concerted action in Western Europe, and strong enough to make its voice sound impressive. In such circumstances it is shortsighted of the United States to act so often like a superpower with a swollen head. What is said here of France might well be said also of Yugoslavia and Vietnam, which have both proved troublesome to their respective superpowers, but also strong and self-reliant.

'Swollen head' is not the most courteous term to use about great countries, yet the nuclear diplomacy of the United States and the Soviet Union (and perhaps in due course of China) often seems to justify it. The failure of the two superpowers to reduce their own nuclear arsenals, while calling on others not to have arsenals at all, readily induces the complaint that they are both vainglorious and hypocritical. In effect, their mutual suspicion causes them not to reduce their nuclear armaments, but in some measure to reduce the rate of growth and of variation in them; this still leaves a vast area of danger for other countries which, if the superpowers had their way, no other state would be allowed to affect by increasing the range of possibilities of deterrence.

IV

The international economy displays much that is ironic. A particular source of irony is the discussion of international trade. States which profess a devotion to free enterprise, such as the United States and Japan, are convinced in practice that it stops at the water line, and that foreigners must not be allowed to reap benefits in their domestic markets if a strong local interest is likely to be hurt. Both countries, for example, are adept at agricultural protectionism, while Japan, which constantly preaches free trade to others, has long been famous for its intricate non-tariff barriers which deter the foreign exporter of manufactures.

Adam Smith and his successors knew quite well that there was no logical difference between free enterprise and free trade; if one were intellectually committed to the first, one would be bound to accept the second. There were exceptions to both, such as defence, which could hardly be run by competing private firms, and infant industries, which to John Stuart Mill seemed to deserve some temporary help from governments; but the two principles hung together. To most Western economists, they seem still to do so; but businessmen and politicians who embrace free enterprise as a slogan are rarely prepared to extend it to free trade in those cases in which profits and employment seem to be in jeopardy. Farmers are even more obviously committed to free trade for their own products but not for those of other countries. Such influences often make international negotiation a game of put and take. States are likely either to start with exceptions and proceed cautiously towards freer trade in those products which do not seem to be at risk, or to start flamboyantly with declarations of free trade, and then produce so many exceptions that the principle is lost to sight.

Communist regimes are no exception to the rule that rhetoric about trade needs to be scrutinised to see if it applies to the point at issue. Their domestic economic propaganda normally minimises the importance of foreign trade, stressing instead the capacity of a socialist economy to generate its own skills, savings and other resources needed for a largely self-sufficient condition involving rising standards of living. Statements about foreign trade (especially in the Soviet Union and Eastern Europe — China has been a refreshing exception in recent years) normally stress the exchanges between socialist countries, which are assumed to share resources equitably and in ways which stimulate economic growth. Yet economic intercourse between the western and eastern halves of Europe has grown rapidly, and capitalist firms have been able to make deals with nearly all the communist regimes. In such cases the customary rhetoric is absent; the managers usually understand one another's points of view; and mutual profit is seen as an obvious and desirable end. Capitalism is one thing in the abstract, a valuable object to blame for one's problems and to incite one's people against. In concrete terms it is often the possessor of valued skills, knowledge and investable funds, and can be brought to a negotiating table.

V

The new states of the Third World also contribute to the multiple ironies of the international system. In the early simple ideology put together for them by Jawaharlal Nehru, they were essentially peace-loving and unacquisitive, and still largely untouched by the aggressive and exploitative habits of European states, which were addicted to power politics. Europe had despoiled their economies but had not managed to destroy their sense of cooperation and mutual understanding. They were, he felt, naturally inclined towards freedom because they had struggled so hard to achieve liberation from their colonial masters. Such an attitude is still to be found, and indeed forms the moral basis upon which the claims for an NIEO are argued.

The ironies arise largely from the fact that, while the leaders of the new states would often like to follow the Nehru precepts and show a forgiving and self-abnegating face to the world, they have grave problems which do not respond to this kind of behaviour, and their peoples are usually not cast in the Gandhian mould from which Nehru drew his model. As with the superpowers and the communist states, ideology is often one thing and practice another. In the case of the new states, the ideology has been extended and systematised by the series of Afro-Asian and 'non-aligned' conferences, and by the formation of the Group of 77 at the UN. What began as a somewhat wistful description of a hoped-for condition has become a public relations exercise designed to hold together a disparate coalition. As with so much that we consider in this essay, there is still some reality behind the rhetoric; but it has been processed to the point at which its credibility is badly strained, and its acceptability is a matter of calculation, rather than of recognition of what is the case.

One of the least attractive but most understandable of Third-World attitudes has been that liberation involves subject peoples struggling to be free from Western dominance, but applies to no other situation. The vast extension of the Russian empire in the nineteenth century, to embrace subject peoples in Central Asia and what is now the Soviet Far East, is dismissed without discussion. More to the point any attempt by a recognisable minority to attain statehood, as with the Kurds, Croats, Biafrans, Ukrainians and those on the fringes of India, is also dismissed. This is largely out of fear of the possible consequences if the existing frontiers of Third-World states were disturbed, and the way laid open yet again for the formation of new states.

The case of the Kurds is especially illuminating. They claim land which is part of Iran, Iraq, Turkey and Syria, which ensures a powerful coalition against them. The UN will not listen to them; neither will the various non-aligned conferences. Their existence calls into question much of the basis on which the ideology of 'liberation' rests. Part of that basis, the assumption of Western exploitation, applies hardly at all to the Kurds. The other part, the assumption that peoples have a right to self-determination, is violated by every state that refuses to acknowledge that the Kurds have a case to be answered. The irony is that each new state looks to the safety of its own ill-designed colonial boundaries when deciding whether the Kurds should have any boundaries at all. In effect, the response of the new states is that self-determination stopped dead when they got the boundaries which they now have and intend to preserve. No new 'national' revolts need occur, and no new 'national' movements' need apply, unless they are located in the remnants of former West European empires. There is nothing universal about such an attitude; instead, it is a rationalisation of a particular set of circumstances, and leads to what all would agree, in the abstract, to be acts of injustice.

A further irony arises from the attachment of new states to universal denunciations of Western colonialism. It is that most ex-colonies seek help, and continue to derive standards, from the former colonial masters which, in accordance with the ideology to which they subscribe, they should be happy to do without. This is especially true of the former French colonies in Africa, but has some relevance also for former dependencies of Britain, and in a lesser degree for the Philippines and Indonesia in respect of the United States and the Netherlands. The elites of these new states seem happy to damn the former colonial powers in the abstract while in concrete terms depending on them for standards in law, education and other fields, and seeking special favours from them in the way of development assistance. There are attractions about the institutions and lifestyles of the former colonial powers which are difficult for the elites of the francophone and anglophone states to resist.

A special case of this tendency occurs in the economic field. Former colonies are happy to demand generalised concessions from the Western world in terms of the NIEO, but often their immediate impulse is to seek special arrangements with the former colonial powers. The arrangements by the EEC under the Lomé Convention and its successors are of special interest in this regard. Originally the result of pressure from France with its own colonies in Africa in mind, these are now concerned with former French, Belgian, Dutch and British colonies in Africa, the Caribbean and the Pacific. The concessions extend beyond aid to the stabilisation of returns from export commodities. The arrangements are complex and far-reaching; but they do not apply to any of those other Third-World countries with which the former colonies are supposed, at UNCTAD and elsewhere, to make common cause.

In practice, the solidarity of the so-called Group of 77 is easily broken, if some developed country has an attractive deal to offer. Some members of the Group are openly cynical about its global objectives, and see no reason to avoid seeking their own advantage while finding the Group a useful rhetorical base from which to operate. In this way the NIEO represents a kind of orthodoxy within which a state can shelter, while rejecting in practice that sense of cooperation and mutual understanding which Nehru prized so highly.

A deeper irony shows itself when new states have to decide whether to give meaning to notions of 'freedom' and 'liberation' in choosing their international associates. They have found that in practice it is difficult to confine associates to those of like mind with themselves. There are usually very few of these. The habits which they have had to acquire have been those of working out whether certain states were actually or potentially hostile, whether others would be likely to support those which they regarded as their enemies, whether certain states were likely to support them in times of crisis and whether their general interests might be harmed by connection with this state or that. Such an analysis has often placed them alongside states which in terms of basic political attitudes might seem poles apart from them.

In this respect the relations between India and the Soviet Union are instructive. While the parties controlling the Indian government since independence have been opposed to the Indian Communist Party in its various forms, and have often attacked it as controlled from abroad (i.e., from the Soviet Union), they have found the Soviet Union an acceptable associate internationally. This is not because of any special sympathy with Soviet aims and practices, but largely because of the persistent antipathy between India and Pakistan, and the fact that Pakistan sought and received arms support from the United States. Since the Soviet Union wished to resist American influence in South Asia, it was happy to be friendly with India. Later conflicts between India and China, when China had distanced itself from the Soviet Union, made the Indo-Russian connection more secure. Almost automatically, Pakistan and China drew closer together, in spite of their markedly different social systems.

Another illuminating case is that of new states' attitudes towards Israel. Rather more complicated in some respects than the South Asian one, it shows how forms of power politics can develop amongst Third-

World states, without the threat of military force. In some respects, it might have been expected that Israel would have good relations with new states emerging from the colonial empires. It was a working democracy; in London and Paris, where much anti-colonial activity had been centred, it was supported by much the same people (of the moderate and sometimes extreme Left) as helped with that activity; it had knowledge and skills to offer; its most prominent politicians were socialists; and, while it was opposed by the existing Arab states, these were not especially attractive to most of those seeking 'liberation' in other parts of the world. For a while Israel managed to remain on good terms with numbers of the new states, especially in Africa; but gradually Arab influence became stronger, more persuasive and harder for the newest states to resist. To Arab influence in the non-aligned movement and the Group of 77 was added Arab economic aid to some of the developing countries. To an increasing extent, the non-aligned ideology became identified with support for the Palestinian Liberation Organisation, and with denunciation of Zionism as a form of racism.

It is hard to believe that many of those states supporting anti-Israel motions at the UN and in other forums were deeply concerned about the Palestinians; they were not concerned about other minorities with as good a claim to self-determination. What they were understandably concerned about was that they might suffer ostracism, vilification and the loss of Arab money if they did not vote for resolutions which were, in any case, matters of verbiage rather than action. It is both significant and ironic that India under Nehru had failed to recognise Israel from the first, and had heavily cultivated the Arab states. A substantial Muslim minority in India, which needed to be placated, and the existence of Pakistan, which might pre-empt the sympathy of these Muslims unless the Indian government showed itself *plus royaliste que le roi*, were amongst the reasons.

One can link with the rise of the new states some, though not all, of the ironies which arise in the operation of international organisations, especially the UN. As suggested in Essay 8, these are bodies inherently liable to be misunderstood because of the common belief that they express 'the conscience of mankind' or the consensus of 'the international community'. This is indeed true when they, like any other assembly, pass resolutions deploring pollution or commending motherhood; when there is nothing to disagree about, they record consensus. Mostly, however, their resolutions are the product of negotiation and compromise between conflicting interests, whether those of individual states or those of groups such as the Arabs, the Africans, the Latin Americans and ASEAN.

Through such horse-trading, which is itself fully legitimate politics, a Third-World position often emerges and is then adopted by Third-World states at large, and by those other states which consider that their interests might be damaged by opposing the Third World. This state of affairs, which has long been characteristic of the UN General Assembly, has also become normal in the Security Council, which is treated by the major powers as no longer significant in terms of possible action. Their practice is to accede on most issues to resolutions expressing a Third-World position, and then to conduct their own business in private. They have largely given up the pretence that security is the province of the Security Council.

It is ironic in the extreme that the UN should retain so many of the trappings and so much of the language of a security organisation, when nobody of international consequence expects it to think as one or act as one — indeed, hardly to act at all. When so-called peace-keeping forces are dispatched to the Middle East and elsewhere, it is usually because this meets the demands of one or another side for some sort of activity, and because the superpowers have satisfied themselves that they will suffer no harm from such an operation.

VI

Irony is an elusive concept. Ironists in literature have been relatively few and sometimes misunderstood. Irony is aroused when people's actions and statements conflict, when events seem to conspire to lampoon the serious efforts of those who embark on a particular course, when there is a marked contrast between pretensions and achievements, when the present replaces the assumptions of the past and when the unexpected and unintended disturb a planned outcome.

The man in the street does not enjoy ironic situations, unless they work to his advantage, when they no longer seem ironic. Confronted with a contrast between what is stated and what actually happens, he is inclined to blame those who made the statements, and to accuse them of hypocrisy. In international as in domestic politics, the citizen's sense of moral outrage is easily aroused. Almost instinctively he indicts particular leaders of hypocrisy, and then puts down his newspaper with a feeling of moral superiority.

Often, of course, he is right. While conscious hypocrisy in saying one thing and doing another is probably less frequent than he thinks, there are many situations in which the gap between promise and fulfilment is so wide that it is hypocritical for the political leader not to acknowledge it. The temptation to ignore the outcome, or to pretend that it was what one had in mind all the time, is hard to resist. Yet it is surely a mistake to think that all the ironies mentioned in this essay result from hypocrisy. The explanation is too glib; much more is required. In many cases, hypocrisy is an insufficient explanation because the situations frequently recur, and the behaviour involved is too consistent to be dismissed as the result of individual weakness, folly or wickedness. These qualities in leaders undoubtedly contribute to the complexities and disappointments of international politics, but there is more to the problem than that.

If we return to Aristotle's image of the leaders as fluteplayers and their peoples as flutemakers, mentioned in Essay 4, we may find that the flute-makers have again been at work. Certainly some of the things which arouse irony can be attributed to the delusions and ambitions of the flute-players, but the interests of the flutemakers are also deeply involved. Divergent and contradictory as these interests often are, they seem to be the dominant elements in many of the situations examined here. A variety of urges towards prosperity and security is to be found amongst the people of every state. These urges lead to contradictory policies which involve freedom for local but not for foreign economic interests, cordial connections with former colonial masters by some sections of the elite while others denounce them, rapidly re-established trade relations with ex-enemies, economic agreements with countries formally described as beyond the pale and so on. It is of the essence of domestic politics that different sections see national prosperity and security in different ways, and each is likely to demand that its case be heeded. There may be great difficulty in reconciling the various interests; something will have to give.

Since this can hardly be spelt out by the foreign minister each time he makes a speech, and would be unpalatable to his supporters if he did spell it out, there should be no surprise that the speeches often point in different directions. Since there are differing interests to be represented, a policy which appears to be all-embracing may in fact serve only one interest, and need to be supplemented, modified and even ignored in order to serve others. The Australian ministers who agreed to wheat sales to China, and simultaneously made out that China was inciting revolt in Asia and must be resisted, were not, in their view, acting like hypocrites. They were serving different interests in a complex situation. The flute-makers were calling for different tunes.

It might be objected that the people hardly call for the propaganda and the sacrifices of war, and that these at least are imposed on them by their rulers. Again, this is partly true. Yet one must also take account of the possibility that acquiescence in (and sometimes enthusiasm for) these things is the obverse of the satisfaction which the state provides through its services, its ceremonies and its cultivation of state nationalism. In domestic terms, the state gains the opportunity to impose obligations in return for what it offers; historically speaking, peoples have normally responded even though the ultimate outcome might be ironically sad in the extreme. Irony is, in a sense, built into the individual's response to the state.

While many international ironies can be explained by the image of the flutemakers, it is perhaps too inclusive to be left without qualification. To pursue the analogy, sometimes the flutes may be to blame, rather than those who make them. In this context the flutes can be regarded as those resources which the state can bring to bear on the international situation. Many states are too poor to live up to their protestations: some have never had the wealth they need; others have lost it. Alternatively, the economic basis on which a state's policy rests may be built up, and may then assist in expanding the part which the state plays on the world scene, as with Britain, France and Germany in the nineteenth century and the United States in the twentieth.

Again, technological change may undermine the economic basis to an extent which renders a state's claims unreal, and creates a situation essentially ironic in character. There is a savage but amusing story by Kipling in which the modern plight of Portugal is set out in this way.[2] One could assert that much of the responsibility for Britain's humiliation over Suez in the 1950s, and Rhodesia in the 1960s, arose from lack of economic and military strength — from the lack, that is, of a serviceable flute. In such cases one can see states making desperate efforts in pursuit of what they could once regard as normal equipment.

Just as technological change may undermine the basis of assertive state action, so may changes in public opinion. What was once normal behaviour may have become unacceptable; the flutemakers may want different tunes from those which formerly pleased them. This too was part of the reason for the British débâcle at Suez. The ironies come from the attempts of national leaders, and of some interests in the community, to make the present look or feel like the past. In the opposite way, ironies may derive from the rebukes which states that have given up particular practices administer to others which have recently adopted them. The United States has often been guilty of this kind of sanctimoniousness. To rebuke the Soviet Union for doing in Afghanistan what one has often done in Central America and the Caribbean is understandable, excusable and perhaps necessary; but a touch of irony is unavoidable.

Perhaps we need to look, not just at leaders, followers, economics and opinion for the sources of irony, but also at the basis of political activity, i.e., at scarcity. Perhaps ultimate and relative scarcity ensure that there is always likely to be a gap between what is wished for and what is gained. This gap may be closed in particular instances, but cannot be closed in all. It is evident in some of the international situations which incite most passion, such as the contrast in wealth between rich and poor countries. A gap that will not close is likely to create situations in which hypocrisy, propaganda and self-delusion become obligatory and lead to irony piled on irony.

Hardy's Sprit Ironic asked a question that sometimes forces itself on the student of international politics:

> As once a Greek asked I would fain ask too,
> Who knows if all the Spectacle be true,
> Or an illusion of the gods (the Will,
> To wit) some hocus-pocus to fulfil?

and did not get a satisfactory answer.[3]

Notes

1. I am not suggesting that Britain took part in the Vietnam war; but there was vigorous controversy about whether it should support or oppose US participation.

2. Rudyard Kipling, 'Judson and the Empire', in *Many Inventions* (London, 1893). It is sad to think that there may now be people thinking of writing such stories about the British.

3. Thomas Hardy, *The Dynasts* (London, 1910) p. 524.

Australia's foreign policy is an active one, and Australians often discuss their place in the world. This, no doubt, is due to their small population (only 14 millions in a country the size of the United States) and their geographical location near to Asia and far from the countries from which they drew their traditions and their high standard of living, which contrasts so markedly with those of their Asian neighbours, and is, to a large extent, based on foreign trade.

The economic content of Australian foreign policy is indeed high, but the state has shown itself abroad to be more than an economic animal. It has frequently been concerned about issues of peace and war (e.g., in 1980 over Afghanistan), and about its own security. Australia is part of the West, whether one views 'the West' in terms of culture, of interlocking alliances or of high standards of living; yet it has been much concerned for over thirty years with the new states of Asia and the Pacific. It is perhaps a useful test case for some of the propositions advanced in previous essays.

I

A brief account of the development of Australia's foreign policy must stress the differences between approaches to the world before and after World War II. The fall of Singapore was, to a large extent, the watershed in official external behaviour.

Before the war Australia was very much preoccupied with Britain, for reasons derived from immigration, trade and defence. Nearly all its people had come from the British Isles; it had deliberately got rid of Asian immigrants at the beginning of the century, and had only slight experience of immigrants from continental Europe. Its export industries, with the exception of wool and minerals, had been built up with the expectation that Britain would be an indulgent customer. Defence had been a matter of reliance on British naval power. Loyalty to Britain was still a powerful element in society, and the proclaimed sentiment of the parties most often in office. Relations with other countries were not of much importance, since British policy was what seemed to matter most. There was little specific interest in Asia, except for apprehension about Japan; a recurrent theme in Australian popular thinking had been a fear of Asian hordes, with Japan as their most likely leader. On the whole, however, Australian horizons were strictly limited, as those, say, of New Caledonia are now. The Japanese thrust in 1941-2 gave substance to the longstanding fear of Asia, inducing for a time a sense of near panic in some people. After Singapore fell, Australia became dependent on the United States for defence.

Since the war, Australian foreign relations have been influenced by a number of developments, both foreign and domestic. The main one, the rise of Russian power, affected all the countries of the West, but had particular significance for Australia because unstable areas in Asia might provide opportunities for Russian power to be extended as it had been in Europe. The appearance of a communist regime in China in 1949 appeared to confirm this danger. For over twenty years thereafter Australia took part in anti-communist wars in Korea and Southeast Asia.

At the same time, Australian governments tried to cultivate the new states of the area by means of diplomacy, development aid and military assistance. The realisation that these were new states and so close, comparatively speaking, to Australia itself, stimulated considerable activity in foreign policy. For a long time the Southeast-Asian horizon was the clearest and most immediate for policy-makers.

The wartime alliance with the United States was renewed in 1951, and still applies. In terms of worldwide issues, Australia has normally followed the American lead. When the United States became actively involved in the Vietnam war, Australia and New Zealand were the only Western states to send troops in support. Australian policy towards China followed the American in most respects, including the failure to recognise the regime until 1972. However, when China's opposition to the Soviet Union was joined by the expressed intention to cultivate relations with the West, Australia responded eagerly.

Domestic changes which directly affected Australian external official behaviour included a postwar immigration policy which admitted large numbers from continental Europe, and later from the Middle East and Asia, as well as from Britain. Another was the development in the 1960s of mineral discoveries which made Australia one of the world's major exporters of iron ore, bauxite, coal and potentially of uranium. Minerals became the biggest source of export income. The direction of Australian trade swung away from Britain and towards Japan, the United States and Southeast Asia. Britain's concentration on Western Europe coincided

with this development. There was a similar shift in the sources of investment from overseas.

Such a brief summary hardly does justice to the changes in Australian
foreign policy. In particular, it does not mention the subtle changes in
attitude which have made the Union Jack almost a foreign flag yet Queen
Elizabeth still welcome as Queen of Australia.

Some questions about this experience, in the light of preceding essays,
are as follows:

— how does foreign policy arise, especially in the balance between
   domestic and foreign influences?
— how are the economic and political elements mixed in foreign
   policy?
— is there any movement towards regional integration?
— how is interdependence understood?
— what part is played in international organisations?
— how, if at all, is soveriegn status threatened?

II

To ask how foreign policy arises in Australia is to invite a simple answer:
that it arises like other sorts of policy but with a smaller input from
organised interests (except in the vastly important sphere of trade policy),
somewhat less from ministers, and rather more from officials. The
answer would be true, but it needs supplementing from abroad. The
significance of the US alliance, the British connection and association
with Japan and the ASEAN states, has been considerable. It has been
regarded as axiomatic that Australian initiatives need to be cleared with
any of these countries that might be affected. Decisions by Australia's
friends abroad (especially by those whom Sir Robert Menzies was
credited with calling 'our great and powerful friends') have been
approved, defended and hardly ever criticised. There is thus an extra
dimension to Australian policy, going beyond the influences present in
Australia itself; it is not just the external dimension as such, but the
dimension of alliance and association. To change the metaphor, this has
constituted a series of horizons of great importance.

A further guide to action has been ideology. Australians are anti-
communist in domestic terms (the communist parties poll very badly
at elections), and it has seemed natural to be anti-communist abroad. In
the 1950s communism was to most Australians, and certainly to the

government, a seamless garment; communist states were controlled by the Soviet Union, as were communist parties, including the one which operated in Australia. To be anti-communist was to oppose the Soviet Union at home where it caused industrial trouble, and abroad where it encouraged subversion. The successful defiance of Soviet control by Yugoslavia and China took a long time to assimilate; and the later development of Eurocommunism, the fragmentation of Marxist beliefs amongst intellectuals, and the three-way split of the Communist Party of Australia itself, modified but did not eradicate the anti-communist nature of the Liberal and Country parties, those which normally constitute governments. Experience in the Vietnam war, association with the ASEAN countries, and the recent cultivation of China, have tended to shift the emphasis of resistance from communism as such to the Soviet Union. Once again, the main reaction is to Soviet power.

Partly because of the strong ideological elements in government policy, and partly because of an Australian tradition of assistance to major allies in foreign wars, the military aspect of Australian policy has also been important. In effect, the Australian forces were on active service, with brief intermissions, from 1939 to 1972. In between they had served in World War II, the occupation of Japan, the Korean war, the Malayan emergency, the confrontation of Malaysia by Indonesia and the Vietnam war. These military experiences were linked with the development of close defence connections with Malaysia, Singapore and Thailand, later to be extended to Indonesia. Cooperation with New Zealand has always been close.

The trade element, which will be dealt with at greater length in the next section, has also been integral to Australian foreign policy. Efforts to keep trade policy in line with ideology and military connection have not always been successful.

Any answer to the question of how Australian foreign policy arises should include the fact that awareness of how other states have tackled similar problems does not seem to have counted. Other countries which have had the task of 'living with a giant' in the American alliance, for example, include Canada and West European countries such as France, Belgium and West Germany. Australian policy-makers appear to have taken little notice of how these states have approached the task; instead, the Australian horizon has been largely confined to the United States, and to a certain extent to Britain. At the same time, governments often show a lamentable lack of understanding of American political processes. There has been a strong tendency to create a basic political relationship between Australia as an interest and the United States as a form of authority. Australia tried in the 1960s to ensure that US authority was paramount in Southeast Asia, and in the 1980s in the Indian Ocean. In both cases the aim was to create a specific kind of international polity with US authority as the dominant element.

In general, the Australian stance in foreign policy is nationalistic, but, as it were, *small* nationalistic; there is an unstated belief that big states either hurt you (e.g., pre-eminently the USSR, but also, in economic terms, the EEC) or love you (as, it is hoped, the USA does and China will). There is little sign of cool calculation, although officials' submissions sometimes show it. It is inclined to get lost in the political process. Some horizons are still blurred.

III

The question of the mixture of economics and politics is of great importance in Australian external behaviour. The political parties are economically based (the Liberals on business and professional interests, the Country Party on farmers, the Labor Party on trade unionists). Such foreign policy as existed before World War II was economic in character and was hardly involved with the issues of world politics. In the 1900s, 1920s and 1930s, the efforts of Australian governments were directed towards persuading Britain to adopt policies of imperial preference which would provide sheltered markets for such Australian products as butter, meat, cheese, fruits and wine. In the period since World War II, economic diplomacy has been particularly vigorous. Traditional markets have been drastically reduced by Britain's entry into the EEC, while the massive purchase by Japan of Australian minerals has required a variety of arrangements to safeguard local interests. The protectionist urges of the US Congress in respect of beef have called for special attention. There have been quarrels with the ASEAN countries about airline operations, and with the EEC about its habit of dumping surplus foodstuffs in markets which Australia might otherwise hope to gain.

In terms of domestic politics, it could be argued that an Australian Cabinet normally consists of two parties, one of which stresses the welfare of the export industries, while the other is more susceptible to manufacturing interests at home, and may not have the same concern about exports. The Country Party wants other countries to reduce agricultural protectionism in order to admit Australian farm products. It is also anxious that the mining industry should have ample access abroad. With its emphasis on export incomes, it has a weakness for depreciation of the exchange rate. The Liberal Party overlaps to a certain extent, but has a solid concern for locally protected manufacturers, and is wary of the free-trade doctrines urged on it by economists and rural organisations. Under these circumstances an Australian prime minister may find it convenient to be a free trader abroad and a protectionist at home.

As well as their economic preoccupations, the two parties are likely to be concerned with ideological issues. Traditionally, the Country Party is the more anti-communist of the two, but the Liberal Party has gained extra force in this respect from the adherence of refugees from Eastern Europe. On the whole, however, ideology is confined to attacks on political opponents: the two parties tend to leave recommendations about major international issues to ministers, and to give special attention to prime ministerial reports of meetings with the leaders of the United States, Britain, Japan, Western Europe and the Commonwealth countries. In this way Australia is seen as gaining friends and influencing people.

Although the advice which proceeds from these sources may sometimes suggest courses antagonistic to the extension of trade in particular directions, it is rare for economic interests to be subordinated to so-called political interests. The matter of wheat sales to China, mentioned in Essay 6, illustrates the point. The reason does not lie in any special magic possessed by the Country Party — it was not essential in numbers to the Liberal Party between 1975 and 1980 and might not be so again — but in the great importance of primary products in the Australian export trade. Only about 15 or 20 per cent of exports are manufactured goods. The remainder are divided fairly evenly between minerals and farm products. Without these, the Australian balance of payments would be shot to ribbons. People in rural areas number between a fifth and a tenth of those in the cities; in terms of numbers they are insignificant. In terms of contribution to the international economy, however, the cities are insignificant. It is not surprising that the Country Party is often the standard-bearer of external policies eventually adopted as official, such as the refusal in 1980 to ban or reduce exports of food to Iran, because of its continued detention of American hostages.

The distinction between political parties in their comparative emphasis on the economic in foreign policy is reflected amongst officials. The departments of Overseas Trade and Foreign Affairs are old rivals within the governmental system. This does not mean that they always disagree, but they watch one another to see that their respective interests are preserved, and that, in any given issue, the economic and political aspects are both stressed. Another department, the Treasury, is less active in negotiations with particular states, but is likely to be dominant when questions of international investment and the exchange rate are uppermost. The Australian bureaucracy is as much a pluralist factor in foreign policy advice as in any domestic context.

Nevertheless, no matter how weighty may be the advice from Treasury and Trade, or how vague the political considerations brought forward by Foreign Affairs, there is bound to be a mixture of political and economic interests in any major policy adopted by an Australian cabinet. The pressures coming, sometimes indirectly, from allies, adversaries and associates; the ideological concerns; the domestic pressures (e.g., from news media and ethnic groups); the criticisms of the Opposition; the need abroad for consistency of tone and reliability of export supplies — these are all factors of consequence. The days when Australia could concentrate on its strictly economic interests are gone for ever. There is little likelihood that, if there were a change of government, it would cause more than a change of emphasis in the mixture.

IV

If Australia were to be regarded as a test case for hypotheses about regional integration, discussion would centre first on New Zealand, then on the states composing ASEAN. Papua New Guinea, the other close neighbour, is a former Australian colony, which gained its independence only in 1975. Integration is hardly something to be discussed when disintegration has taken place so recently.

Australia and New Zealand appear to be exceptionally suitable for integration. Their peoples derive from much the same origins, speak the same language and are often mistaken for one another when they pronounce it. They enjoy roughly similar standards of living, have similar political traditions and have fought in all the same wars. When the Australian colonies began to discuss the possibility of federation in the 1890s, New Zealand representatives were present. Since early in the century, New Zealand regular army officers have been trained in Australia's Royal Military College, Duntroon. The two countries are allied with the United States by the ANZUS Treaty, and share in American intelligence activity. Each allows the other's citizens to enter freely without passports.

In spite of these aspects of the relationship, which would seem favourable towards closer connection, progress towards anything approaching integration has been slow. The two countries' economies developed to a certain extent along parallel lines, which made them competitors in foreign markets for wool, meat and dairy products. New Zealand manufacturers, protected like their Australian counterparts, had a much smaller home market to fill, and so most could not achieve the economies of scale available in the bigger market in Australia. There has consequently been pressure from agricultural interests on the Australian side to protect those products, such as lamb and butter, which New Zealand could produce more cheaply; and similar pressure from manufacturing interests in New Zealand which saw themselves swamped if all Australian products were free to move in. A so-called free-trade area (a GATT name for an arrangement not meaning quite what the name would suggest) between the two countries has been established, but has not affected the basic problem of competing industries, each of which wields considerable political power in its own country.

When one considers that the two states are closely associated in defence and foreign policy, that their peoples can vote in one another's elections when resident and show a natural affinity towards one another when they go abroad, and that some of the two governments' expenditure entails duplication of services which could advantageously be brought together (e.g., in education, research, defence, diplomacy), there would seem to be a strong case for integration. Policies of structural readjustment of the two economies (likely to be pursued in any case) could in time modify the problem of competing industries. Would the two states be likely then to integrate with one another?

Two major problems would certainly intrude. One is that, while it would not be constitutionally difficult to have New Zealand become an additional state within the existing Australian federal structure, this would not be likely to satisfy the New Zealanders, amongst whom the demand for equal status with Australia in some new political unit — a sort of union of crowns — would probably be strong. They would, after all, be giving up sovereign equality to accept non-sovereign inequality in the existing Australian federation. Australians, on the other hand, would probably not wish to give the 3 million New Zealanders equal status as a group with the 14 million of themselves. There are two Australian states, New South Wales and Victoria, each of which has more people than New Zealand.

This problem of constitutional status is linked with an even greater problem, that of national identity. New Zealand has been a sovereign state for a long time, and had many of the habiliments of one for even longer.[1] While inclined for longer than Australians to call themselves British, New Zealanders have had a very clear sense of the individuality of their land, and of their particular ways of doing things. They have developed their own systems in politics, law, government, education, farming and so on. These systems are close to the Australian, but still distinct. Any form of integration would involve problems of compatibility of laws, personal status, career structures, professional attitudes, forms of organisation, and day-to-day discourse — the kinds of things which contribute to national identity.

A variety of interests would be seriously affected, but the principal interest would be that which New Zealanders have acquired through possessing and operating a sovereign state of their own. To become a state of the Commonwealth of Australia would not be at all the same thing. New Zealanders are attached to their institutions. Their state, while not a demonstrative one, is an object of pride for many of them. They have no particular attachment to Australia, and are often critical of Australians — who, for that matter, are often critical of them. The two states have by now their two separate identities, which it would probably be very difficult to merge.

The ASEAN case is, as it were, in a different dimension. Australia has cultural and linguistic compatibility with only a small minority of people in ASEAN; nobody is likely to propose full integration, such as is often suggested for New Zealand. Instead, the suggestion is to move closer together in policy, especially trade policy, and to avoid actions which might go against one another's interests.

While it is clear that Australia has similarities in outlook internationally to most of the ASEAN countries, and would like to gain further from connection with the dynamic growth of their economies, there are major difficulties to surmount. The most obvious of these in recent years has been the Australian retention of protection for such industries as textiles, clothing and footwear in the face of ASEAN countries' demands that the market be more accessible to their products.

There are also less tangible difficulties, arising from the political and social systems of the five ASEAN countries. Their mutual relationship is fragile, and could be disrupted by changes of policy or social disturbance in only one or two of them. The element of authoritarianism in their governments is substantial, and is hardly likely to lessen. This makes it difficult to solve questions of leadership in the group as a whole, since authoritarian leaders do not like to be seen deferring to one another. Indonesia, which has by far the biggest population and military establishment, regards itself as the natural leader of the group; but its economic development is patchy, and its internal politics might prove volatile at just the time when stable leadership was needed. ASEAN is, in fact, a success for the time being in certain restricted respects; otherwise it is a risk as a partner, and conceivably a liability. It is not surprising that Australian policy-makers should differ about the utility of closer connection.

It may well be that proposals for some sort of Pacific community or organisation for Pacific trade and development will replace schemes for integration with New Zealand and closer links with ASEAN. The most recent of these proposals[2] calls for the kinds of connection which would suit dominant Australian interests in trade, while avoiding the formal entanglements which might cause disruption. It has the further virtue, from an Australian standpoint, of involving Japan, the United States and the Pacific island states.

In general, Australian experience suggests little substance in the idea of regional integration. The New Zealand case shows how similarity can be a problem; the ASEAN case, how dissimilarity can induce caution and perhaps make wider-ranging alternatives more attractive. If there is a 'region' surrounding Australia (and Australian politicians usually say there is, without defining it), the region is not susceptible to political integration. Indeed, it can be argued that increased transactions have led to more tension, rather than to an urge towards unity.

V

What has just been said about integration is linked with the question of how interdependence is seen in Australia. There is no doubt that Australian governments (those of the states as well as the Commonwealth or federal government, which is the effective diplomatic authority) are intensely aware of the country's need for trade with other developed economies, and for investment from them. The future development of oil and minerals is directly dependent on foreign investment, and the country's economic growth upon foreign markets for the mineral exports which that investment will produce. Because the process has been previously successful, Australian governments will go to considerable lengths to get more overseas investment in order to promote employment, industrial diversity and a favourable balance of payments. There are numerous complaints from the Left about the dangers of 'foreign ownership', but these are usually dismissed as empty dogma by ministers. After all, Australia contains many multinational companies, and there is little or no evidence of their trying to take over the country, though they have sometimes objected to what governments wanted them to do.

At the same time, however, Australian governments display a good deal of economic nationalism, notably in respect of overseas investment. In recent years, for example, the Liberal-Country Party government has refused permission for an American company to carry on sand-mining on Fraser Island, off the coast of Queensland; it has attempted to remove from the jurisdiction of the US Anti-trust Act the operations of Australian uranium companies alleged to have joined in a cartel to push up the price of uranium; it has set standards (not always observed) for the degree of Australian equity in mining ventures initiated by foreign investors; and it has been against foreign investment in Australian television companies. It has also shown vigour in protecting Qantas, the Australian international airline, and complained bitterly about agricultural protectionism by Japan, the EEC and the USA, together with the EEC's dumping of surplus farm products.

The tone of Australian economic rhetoric is consistently national — subject, of course, to obligatory obeisances to the abstract ideals of alliance, peace, fair-dealing and international cooperation. Interdependence is essentially something to be praised when it works 'our way'. When it benefits others without benefiting us, or actually makes us seem poorer, it is nothing to be commended. Questions of trade, investment and the exchange rate are normally discussed by politicians as if they concerned nobody but Australia. There are reminders about mutuality and interdependence in newspaper editorials, but the other side of interdependence — the rights of foreigners and the need for trade to be a two-way street — are traditionally stressed only by graziers, importers and economists. Australia may well be unusually stark in its economic nationalism, but it is probably not untypical. No international body purporting to regulate interdependence would get much credence unless it could clearly show that Australia would benefit in specific ways, and that what were regarded as particular Australian interests would be safeguarded.

In this respect, one can point to the question of Antarctica. In 1933 Australia proclaimed authority over that part of Antarctica, excluding Adélie Land between the 160°E and 45°E meridians of longitude. The area was directly south of Australia. The claim has never been formally recognised by a number of states, including the USA, but in 1959 an international conference of 12 interested states drew up a special Antarctic treaty, which is still in force. In spite of widespread suggestions that Antarctica should become global property and be internationally administered in the interests of mankind as a whole, Australian policy is to retain the existing portion of Antarctica and to resist any change. Such a policy is a mixture of a determination not to give up what is already 'our own', of vague notions of security and of the idea of possible economic gain, especially from minerals and krill. The existing treaty provides for some international cooperation (e.g., between Australian and Russian scientists), and is regarded as the best in the circumstances. A special international organisation would not be welcomed.

VI

The point just made is generally applicable to participation in international organisations. 'The conscience of mankind' is approved when it is expressed by those states which Australians trust and approve of; in other words, unless international bodies are obviously influenced or controlled by states with which Australia is associated, they are viewed with some suspicion. Even when the UN General Assembly habitually responded to the touch of John Foster Dulles, the Australian government was disturbed by the non-aligned and anti-colonial sentiments expressed in it. When the character of the Assembly began to change in the 1960s, even more concern was shown.

The issues on which the governments of Sir Robert Menzies found the UN wanting included Papua New Guinea (then an Australian dependency, part of which was a UN Trust Territory), Indonesian designs on West Irian, and the Suez crisis of 1956 (one of the very few occasions on which Australia found itself on the opposite side to the United States). In the same period there was anxiety lest the General Assembly criticise the White Australia Policy and Australia's treatment of its aboriginals. Since the end of Sir Robert's reign in 1966, Papua New Guinea has become independent, West Irian has been safely incorporated in Indonesia (which is now highly regarded by the Australian government), the White Australia Policy has been abandoned and there have been no more Suezes. Nevertheless, the aboriginal question remains, and there has been some concern about UN interference in Australia's remaining minuscule colonial possessions. The campaign for an NIEO has caused mixed feelings in the Australian government, since Australia produces a number of primary products, and might possibly benefit from some of the commodity agreements which are envisaged; at the same time, other aspects of the NIEO proposals might be harmful to Australia as an officially 'developed' country and a member of OECD, the developed countries' club.

Ironies have proliferated in Australia's activities at the UN, especially in the government's selective use of incidents from the past to garnish its present performance. For example, the Liberal-Country Party government often speaks in self-congratulatory terms of Australia's assistance with the emergence of Indonesia in the 1940s, in spite of the fact that the actions in question were those of a Labor Party government, against which the Liberal-Country Party opposition strongly protested. Again, Australia began its UN career as a staunch supporter of South Africa on the ground that racial policy was a matter of domestic jurisdiction, the section on which in the UN Charter had been strengthened at the insistence of a Labor minister, Dr H.V. Evatt, with the aim of protecting the White Australia Policy. Now that the policy is a thing of the past, and South Africa so obviously an international pariah, such support has disappeared. Australian participation in the Korean war was justified in terms of its being a UN war; little is said about it now, and the UN is not incited to undertake other wars. There is nothing unique about these ironies; other states which, like Australia, have been members of the UN from the beginning could produce similar stories.

On the whole, in spite of anxieties from time to time, the UN system seems to be regarded by the Australian government as vaguely a good thing provided it sticks to technical efficiency and, in matters of economics and security, to declarations which are not obviously anti-Western. There are signs that sophistication has increased since the Menzies days.[3] There is little suggestion, however, of increasing responsibilities for any UN agency.

VII

In broad terms, the answer to the question whether the sovereign status of Australia is threatened is that the country, whether viewed in terms of public opinion or of the attitudes of its government, sees sovereignty as likely to be threatened only in the old-fashioned way — by conquest. If there were a war between the superpowers, or if some Asian state became both militarily strong and bloody-minded in its ambitions, Australians would fear the loss of their present independence. There is no indication that they fear it from any other direction, i.e., no sign that multinational corporations and international organisations have any chance of taking over functions of government, or that any superstate, created by processes of integration, could usurp Australian sovereignty. Indeed, it is the New Zealanders who fear that, in certain circumstances, Australia might take over their sovereignty. The Australian people show no awareness of problems that have to be solved for them by foreigners because of the inadequacy of their own state.

Just how Australians view their own state is as difficult to discover as in any other case. There is undoubtedly a strong national consciousness. Australians who go abroad are traditionally divided into two categories, those who return with the statement that Australia is the best country in the world after all, and those who say that it has vigour but lacks culture. Any belief that it should import the political institutions of any other state is usually confined to people who were committed to the other state in the first instance. Indeed, it is difficult in the Australian case (and may be very difficult elsewhere) to separate a sense of the state from simple patriotism. Australians identify themselves with the country, and hardly ever speak of 'the state' in the way it has been used in these essays. This is perhaps because the component parts of the Australian federation are called 'states', and a further usage might be confusing. It is also because the state appears to be viewed as very much an instrument of the people. In this sense, the flutemakers think that they are in command.

If foreigners emigrate to Australia, or invest in it, they do so at their own risk. The assimilation of the children of immigrant families is rapid and remarkably thorough. Foreign firms have to meet Australian standards, accept Australian trade unions, and pay Australian taxes after whatever initial honeymoon may have been devised for them. As already suggested, foreign investment is eagerly sought, but foreign enclaves are not encouraged. The treatment of foreign firms is calculated largely in terms of what might attract or repel foreign investors in the future; there is no desire to kill the goose that lays the golden eggs, but the goose becomes a domestic animal none the less.

In fact, Australian sovereign status is threatened by nothing and nobody. Conquest is a remote possibility which must never be entirely disregarded, but otherwise there is no threat. Here is a state to which its people see no alternative, however much they may at times wish to change domestic details, and which past experience suggests they would fight to preserve. Are other states so different?

Notes

1. New Zealand has governed itself for over a hundred years, but New Zealand leaders in the 1920s strenuously resisted the proposition that the British Dominions, of which New Zealand was one, were sovereign states, in spite of their membership of the League of Nations. This sort of obfuscation was abandoned in the 1940s, but there is no date on which New Zealand (or Australia) could be said to have become 'independent'.

2. A proposal by Peter Drysdale and Hugh Patrick is to be found in *An Asian-Pacific Regional Economic Organization: An Exploratory Concept Paper* prepared for the Committee on Foreign Relations, US Senate, by Congressional Research Service, July 1979 (US Government Printing Office, Washington, 1979), Document 46-192.

3. See especially *Australia and the Third World: Report of the Committee on Australia's Relations with the Third World* (Canberra, 1979).

INDEX